IN ANOTHER LIFE

A Novel

Meg Oliver

In Another Life

ISBN Number: 978-0-6151-7461-7

Acknowledgments

My mother always taught me to say "thank you." She also taught me to love books. My grandparents, Doots and Si Oliver taught me about unconditional love and family. They believed in me. So did my Aunt Norma who bought my first horse and taught me about unselfishness.

Thank you to Tony Turner, my High School Creative Writing teacher who taught me how much fun writing can be. Thank you to Barbee Griffis and Cynthia Kachik for being my life-long friends. To Lisa Ray, Kim Leiby, Cindy Schneider, and Kim Storey for embracing me as your friend in recent years. You have all given me hope. To Angela Hall for reading each page as I wrote it, and for your love.

Jack Oleson's computer expertise kept me from losing my mind. Thank you for always smiling. Thank you to fellow writers Sheldon Siegel and Gwen Hunter for your professional advice.

Most of all, I want to thank my family, Calin and Kielee O'Brien. Thank you, Calin, for helping me to believe in true love and family… and always.

ONE: Moving

It was really happening. Twenty years is long enough to live
in one house, anyway. "Sandra Elizabeth Greene!" I'd called
my own name out loud and my voice suddenly sounded like
my mother's. "Just exactly what do you think you're doing
young lady?" Again, I heard my voice, so I answered in my
head. This was all happening because I was orchestrating it.
Unlike my mother, I had the courage to design and implement
turning my life upside down—on purpose. She had lived in
the same house since I was five years old. Life had always
been thrust upon her unwillingly: Children, divorce, work,
and so forth, and so on. Dependant mentality dictated the
choreography to which she danced. Not me. Not ever!
But for an instant, I considered putting the house key back in
my own pocket instead of into the outstretched hands of the
couple that were about to take possession of "my house." I
could simply instruct the movers to unload the moving van.
They had adequate muscle mass for the task, and I would
obviously pay them for their time and effort. Money wasn't a
problem. Motorola would take me back. After all, I had been
their top salesperson for the last seven years in a row. At forty-
two, they'd buy my mid-life crisis excuse and simply tear up
the well-worded letter of resignation I had submitted. "NO
WAY!" I was thinking out loud again.

The Sassers thought I was talking to them. "What? Sandy, are
you all right?" Until now, this young couple with a two-year-
old son had only seen me in business mode. Now they were
experiencing my panicked one-hundred-mile-per-hour
misgivings about quitting my job, selling my house, and
moving to Georgia.

"Good luck with the house, kids," I muttered as I pressed the
key into an eager hand. There are few moments in this life
when your heart and stomach align to produce that exact
mixture of emotions. Both taking possession of your first
house and surrendering a 'home' to virtual strangers produce
that self-same mix. I had not planned anything original or
poetic to say. That was obvious. I just left.

"You have the directions?" I quizzed the head mover.

"Yep," lulled his eloquent reply. "I gottem. See you down south, y'all." It always irritated me when people used the word "y'all" referring to only one person. But then again, my roommate in college had said the one thing she learned from me was the plural of y'all was "all of y'all". I wondered what comments he voiced about me to his co-pilot as he nosed the eighteen-wheeler, which now contained my life in boxes, down the driveway of what was no longer my home.

After a long look back, I hit the gas and made my way through familiar streets. My Isuzu Trooper was packed perfectly, mostly with meowing cats. Their chorus from the cat carriers made me wonder what they were saying. After a few hours they'd stop...at least, I hoped they had. It not, this could be a very long trip!

Columbus, Ohio. The place hardly sounds this difficult to leave. It is understandable to feel the loss of a home and a good job, but a city hardly warms one's heart. Especially a city in the Midwest! When I first moved to Ohio, I had thought it would put me closer to my friend in Colorado. It wouldn't be humid either, I had presumed. Neither geography nor meteorology was my field of expertise—obviously. Yet now, as I wove through streets with my own internal North Star guidance system, I realized the comfort of the familiar. And here I was leaving all that behind as I drove.

Clintonville, my section of the city, was close to everything. Ohio State University, hospitals, shopping centers, downtown, the freeway, and the restaurants. The Olentangy Inn. Would anyone realize that this restaurant had the best Chinese food in town? Their origami "to go" containers released food that transformed my home into another culture altogether. I ate it all with authentic chopsticks that had been a present from the Presbyterian minister when I was twelve years old. He'd been to Japan as a missionary and I wondered often if he even realized I still had the chopsticks or that I used them religiously.

Clothes might not make the man, but food definitely does make the city! At least that is my view of it all, anyway. Pizzario Uno wasn't in Clintonville, but a worn path led there from my house. The only Long Island Iced Tea worth drinking was a relaxing diversion while my spinnocoli deep-dish pizza was being prepared. My ex-husband didn't like pizza. That should have been a red flag. "How could anyone not like pizza?" Again, I found myself thinking aloud. The cats, however, didn't think this as weird as others I had encountered in my day. That could be because they were busy doing the same.

Another thing I was sure to miss was a theater where you could watch the latest movie on the big screen while drinking beer and eating pizza. Life should always be so complete. However, I'm reasonably sure they will have cool unique things, places, and food where I'm headed. It is the south, after all, and the state where I was raised. Interstate 71 was now taking me steadily in that direction. It was really happening!

Maybe I would visit. Maybe not. I had a new chapter to write in my life. This I knew. If we do nothing to change our lives today, they will be the same tomorrow as they were yesterday. Not sure where I heard that, or who said it first, but it struck a chord with me. I admired the same courage and spontaneity in me that my mother envied yet despised.

I'm off. I'm scared to death. I am excited beyond explanation with the anticipation of new places, new friends, and new places to eat and grow— figuratively not literally. Comfortable familiarity will form new neurological pathways where I'm bound. And I know they have pizza there. Plus they have hot boiled peanuts in small brown paper bags for sale along the highway at roadside stands.

I needed to drive faster. The moving van had a substantial head start.

TWO: Motelling It

When the backseat feline choir settled in for a long drives' nap, the trip steadily grew longer as I drove. The herd of deer that grazed undauntedly on the edge of the freeway convinced me though. One of the herd decided the smorgasbord must continue on the other side of the interstate, so he gracefully bounded across the concrete obstruction in his meal. I barely missed him, and the rest of his dinner companions never knew that a large metal bullet had whizzed dangerously past them all as they ate. Time for a hotel room.

The next exit had several choices, but I chose the one that seemed most likely to be American-owned. I will never understand why so many people from India aspire to own and run hotels in this country, or why our government chooses to give all the tax breaks to foreigners, but it upsets me. Anyway, I found a room and brought in my small overnight bag. Then I threw a small blanket over the cat carriers and unabashedly carried them into the room as if they were suitcases. Doesn't everyone put a blanket over his or her suitcase when it is drafty outside? The traveling litter box came next, and I locked the door behind us all. My traveling companions explored, meowed, and meowed some more. I wondered if the people next door or the management or the whole world could hear the cacophony.

Why is there so much static electricity in motel rooms? A cat finally settled in next to me and instead of a comforting stroke on the back, I shocked her. Murphy looked back at me with disdain. She was unaware of the naturally occurring phenomenon of static electricity, and blamed me instead. But she came back. She liked to nuzzle up in that space behind my knees.

As I drifted off to sleep in strange surroundings, I wondered how far the moving company had gone. They were men, so I was certain they were in mortal combat with the road. But maybe they'd get lost. With men, there was always that possibility. And since they would never dream of asking directions, maybe I could make up any lost ground in the morning.

I awoke with a start. Time to go! Even though I was certain the movers would get lost, time was still at a premium. I fed the cats some soft cat food and quickly threw on my traveling clothes. It felt like a vacation to start the day in jeans and hiking boots, but the only mountains I had to climb were in my lifestyle. I could easily get used to this, though. No starched suits, no panty hose, and no pumps. And no sales quotas or cranky customers or traffic jams. Free at last, free at last!

After throwing on my clothes and returning the cats to the car, we refueled and were on our way. Strong coffee will always be an integral part of my morning and this was no exception. The more I drank from my thermos bottle, the faster I seemed to drive. My meowing travel companions vocalized the excitement I felt about arriving at our new home and beginning another life. They were used to me leaving home early in the morning for my daily three-mile run. Later I would return home, shower, dress, and head for my office. When I returned home, it would be dark. The office wasn't a corporate one. It was my idea. Motorola allowed me to work from home, but there were too many personal distractions, and an office felt more focused and professional. Worthington was a nearby suburb that had a British feel. My little office was close to the outer belt and there were restaurants nearby—food for fuel or for business meetings. I would miss my clients. Taking people out to lunch on my expense account was fun. I would probably miss that as well. As I pondered the changes I had set in motion for myself, I knew I was ready. The corporate life was a skill I had mastered. I could do all that in my sleep, and without the challenge it had become boring to me. And so what if everyone in the known world had a pager and a cell phone? I was ready for a new type of connections…one to my neighbors, and to the earth, and to my roots, to horses, and to myself. I had already found myself. Now I planned to free myself.

THREE: Unpacking

Each time I turned in the key to a motel room where I had harbored undeclared pets, I felt the same. But this time was uneventful like its predecessors. No hidden camera had observed either their secreted entrance or exit. No neighbor reported meowing. I got away scot-free! This did nothing to restore my fear of the "NO PETS" signs that graced many a front desk. I was a hardened criminal on the road again.

The moving truck had won the contest. This came as no surprise to me, but I still dreaded the attitude that I knew would roll out of the cab along with the burley men who welcomed my arrival. They were being paid…paid for sleeping at this point. I was determined that nothing nor nobody could nobody ruin my mood d'jour. After all, if I had no man to carry me over the threshold of my new home, my soaring spirits would carry me over alone.

"Glad you could join us, Missie," the mover further revealed his lack of diplomacy.

"Any trouble with the directions?" was my reply, as I ignored the jab about my tardiness.

"Nope. Piece of cake," was his answer, although I was certain these men would give up national security secrets before admitting that they had gotten lost. They were here and I unlocked the door of my cabin so they could bring my life in boxes into its new dwelling. I felt so excited and so in change and so alone. But that could change, and had to be the least of my cares.

Each box was carefully labeled and relegated to a specific room. Rooms had been sketched from photos in my memories. Order gave comfort to chaos-even the controlled chaos of moving. It would take me no time to unpack. The realization that I didn't have to go to work brought relief and an added twinge of fear. It had been years since I wasn't living under the constraints of the daily grind. My mind wasn't yet used to the fact that I was my own boss and no longer a slave to a schedule or a career or a clock. It would take time to redefine time. My new life was off to a great start.

In Another Life

Unloading seemed to take no time at all. My "IMMEDIATE NEEDS" box was such a good idea: coffee and coffee accoutrements, toilet paper, paper towels, and napkins, a flashlight, light bulbs and candles. Coffee, paper, and light. My needs were simple. I would unpack the house systematically—kitchen first. It seemed strange to see my belongings filling this cabin I had only visited as a child. I had always hated to leave comforts of this family cabin. Now I would call it home.

FOUR: Neighbors

Someone was knocking. The horseshoe doorknocker heralded the arrival of my first houseguest. Habit caused me to look through the peephole before opening the door. Through it, I saw a scrubbed wholesome cherub face complete with an irresistibly disarming smile. As soon as the door opened, my new neighbor introduced herself.

"Hi Neighbor, I'm Rebecca Sensenbrenner. My husband Tim and I live right over there in the house with the green shutters. Tim is at work, but I wanted to come over right away and welcome you. Here is some rosemary bread I baked for you and some olive oil to dazzle on it. And I hope you like a good Chardonnay. I thought a christening of your new home would be appropriate and breaking bread with a neighbor would be a bonding time."

As I ushered the cherub into my house, instincts told me it would be the beginning of a life-altering and permanent friendship. What a thoughtful gesture!

"You aren't going to believe this, but you just happened to have picked my favorite wine, Rebecca." As I found the corkscrew and addressed the bottle of Rodney Strong Chardonnay, she insisted that I call her Becca.

"Will you join me, Becca?"

"Absolutely, we have christening ahead of us!"

Wine in paper cups was never so ordinary or inappropriate.

"So, when will your horses arrive? News travels quickly in small towns, you know?"

In an odd way, it was comforting to realize that my new neighbors already knew all about me. Many of them know my folks since the cabin had been in my family for generations during its stint as a vacation spot. Now, it seems they also know my pets.

"The horse transport company will deliver them tomorrow afternoon. That affords me time in the morning to set up the corrals." As I revealed the schedule of events to my new neighbor, I was secretly proud of my organizational skills.

"Great! Tim is off work tomorrow and we will help you set up the corrals. With three of us it shouldn't take any time at all." My new neighbor began unveiling her modus opperandi: she was determined to become my good friend and her thoughtful helpful generous nature seemed to insure success in that regard.

"And we can go pick up the supplies in our flatbed to save the delivery charge, if you want. I'm off work today and tomorrow too. I work as a surgical nurse at Mills Memorial Hospital."

So she is smart, accomplished, thoughtful, and a good cook. Tim must be a lucky man. From what I had gleaned about my neighbor thus far, Becca was a remarkable woman whose wholesome appearance and track record of kindness made it hard to guess her age. Somewhere in her early fifties would be my guess though.

"Do you have horses?"

"Absolutely. We have two Appaloosas. You will have to come over and meet them later when you're ready for a break. We don't show or anything. But trail riding is a great pastime. And our mare is bred, so we should have a youngster sometime next month. Your time as the new kid on the block will be short-lived, so you better enjoy the limelight while it's on you." That mischievous grin reminded me of someone. Who was it? After a brief memory search, I remembered. It was I. Long before the daily grind shoved the innate sense of adventure I'd had into the background, I had possessed that same impish expression. Now I could recapture it as Becca obviously had done. That was part of the reason I had decided to move back here. This cabin had always represented freedom and play to me. Now it was time to play again before I forgot how. And I had found a playmate in Becca. No matter how old we get, it is always essential to have a playmate.

"My horses are Arabians. Two mares. I plan to breed them and sell the babies. I do not know all that much about breeding, but I'm going to learn. Since I'm not independently wealthy, I will have to have a means of supporting myself here. I plan to grow my own food and breed horses." I wasn't sure if my master plan had made it to the local grapevine, but it was no state secret, after all. And I could tell that Becca would be my ally in all my adventures including that one.

FIVE: Settling In

Becca stayed and helped me unpack the entire kitchen. Then we sat down and polished off the bottle of wine and another identical one I'd stashed away for the same occasion. The bread with warm olive oil was like eating a spicy warm cloud, and I was feeling so welcomed here with my new friend gracing my home and my dining table. Once the wine glasses were unpacked, we switched from paper cups to Waterford crystal without spilling a drop in the profound leap. I do not normally consume wine in mass quantities, but the more enthusiastically we talked, the faster we seemed to sip.

I told Becca about my decision to change my life, and about the reaction of my family and friends. She admired my courage aloud and vowed to help me in my quest to simplify my life. Henry David Thoreau would be proud of my attempts to live deliberately. And I even had a pond on my property!

After Becca left, I turned the classical music up really really loud and unpacked my bedroom next. Sometimes music is much better at increased volume. It is almost an added mental crescendo. Neatly folded clothes in drawers and shoes aligned on the closet floor made this feel more like a permanent home instead of a vacation cabin. I decided to have a yard sale soon. It would afford me the opportunity to meet more of my neighbors as well as throw off some unneeded ballast. My wardrobe was evolving along with my life and all the business suits with matching pumps and purses had retired even though they were still present.

Since my cupboard was bare, I decided to eat dinner out. Junior's Barbecue had called my name on the way into town. As I ate the barbecued beef and baked beans, I felt at home. The sweet tea washed down a familiar meal that for years I only had while on vacation visiting Mama. Now it was less than five miles from my cabin, and I was destined to become a frequent flier. The dining room was sparsely dotted with people. As I scanned the room, I wondered who all would become my friends. This new life was fun.

En route to my truck, I passed a veterinarian's rig.
Since my horses were arriving the next day, I thought it wise to
scribble down his name and number. "Dr. Clayton
Thompson," I said aloud and decided to call Becca to ask her
opinion. It shouldn't be too late to phone her when I got home.

"Doc Thompson is the vet we use, and he is also the best there
is around here. He graduated from Clemson Vet School and
has been practicing here ever since. He is in his mid-forties,
and specializes in horses. You will like him, I'm sure.
Something wrong with one of your horses?"

"No, Becca. Just preparing for their arrival. Long hauls
sometimes include boo boos. Thanks for the info. See you in
the morning. And thanks again for everything."

SIX: Horses

Morning arrived just as peacefully as did its predecessor.
Coffee and the Today Show were much more humane than the
freeway and cars full of drones on their way to the daily jail
referred to as 'jobs'. During my unfortunate incarceration
along with the rest, I kept thinking there had to be a better way.
This was it. Even though it was still early and I had a busy day
ahead, it was a calm and unhurried start to things. And I was
wearing jeans, tennis shoes, and no makeup yet. Maybe I
would stop wearing makeup altogether. I heard somewhere
that makeup was intended to make a woman's face appear
flushed as it does just after an orgasm. The corporate world,
maybe. But this world had few requirements like that.

I felt beautiful and more alive than I had for years. The horn of
Tim and Becca's Ford flatbed sounded like a foghorn. And the
roar of the diesel engine gave the appearance we were going to
do some serious work. Tim had the cherub look about him as
well. He was a big clean-cut man, and I decided instantly that
if I were trapped in a burning building I would feel confident if
he came to my rescue through the smoke. He was probably a
skilled firefighter and his wife was no doubt a qualified nurse
as well as a culinary expert. After introductions, we headed off
for Pioneer Feed. I'd called to reserve the pipe corrals on the
same day that I made the transporting reservation for the
horses. All my ducks were in a row.

Tim was as gregarious as his wife had been the day before.
And the huge red toolbox on the floorboard in the back seat
showed they had come prepared to work. I had ordered
wrenches for the occasion but ventured a guess that the
Craftsman toolbox at my feet was replete with all the tools we
would need for the occasion.

The folks at Pioneer had the pipe corrals tagged with a
cardboard tag with my name and today's date on them. So did
the feed tubs and water tanks. The word "DELIVER" had been
crossed out in red. After Becca's offer, I had telephoned them
and told them I would pick up the supplies myself. Even
though the delivery charge was only thirty dollars, retrieving

them myself fit in well with my planned self-sufficient lifestyle. I suspected that my new neighbors wouldn't allow me to pay them for their chariot and the work we were about to do. But I would pay them back by having them over for dinner after our work was done. I also intended to go out of my way to help them in similar circumstances. That was a southern habit I missed while living in Ohio…the habit of helping your neighbors and friends just to be neighborly. People in most cities hardly even know their neighbors' names. That was all different here, and I liked this version better.

We loaded the supplies onto the flatbed and Tim fettered them down as if he had operated a delivery service for years. The bright red tie straps matched his firefighter's suspenders. These were a part of his uniform that he wore even on his day off. Plus, they looked more substantial and yet more comfortable than a belt. Unloading the corrals was just as simple and, with the three of us at work, the assembly was accomplished in no time at all. The two twenty-four by twenty-four pipe corrals would give me a place to separate the girls at feeding time. My master plan included fencing off my forty acres for pastures since I do not believe that horses or people should be jailed unless they have committed some sort of crime. Forty acres might still be considered confining to a horse, but it is roomier than most accommodations.

The pasture and corrals were close to and visible from both the living room and master bedroom of my little cabin. I'm not sure why people have horses and house them so far away from their living space. I want them near me so that I can hear them in the middle of the night and so I can see them when I look out most every window. Night noises are familiar and sounds that do not belong stand out. If one of my mares foals or if somebody gets cast under the fence, I want to hear it and run to their rescue. The position of my shiny new corrals is ideal. It is close enough to the house, but not so close that they can chew on the cabin. Now all I needed was to position and fill the water tubs.

We planned to make a second trip to Pioneer after lunch to pick up twenty bales of hay and ten bags of sweet feed. The little shed out back will be perfect as a feed shed until I get the barn built. And I like positioning everything just the way I want. Having horses in my back yard is going to feel so great. Owning horses and boarding them elsewhere feels like having pretend horses. They might have been mine all along on paper, but even though I paid the board bill for many years, they didn't seem like they were really mine. Now we would all be together as families should. And their arrival was rapidly approaching. Three o'clock was just around the corner and I wondered how far away they were in the horse transport semi?

We ate sandwiches from a local deli that fueled our feed run. Bucking hay had amazingly not been part of my daily grind, and my muscles cried out in protest. It felt good to be sore from physical labor, and I was enjoying the outdoors and the company of my new pals. After all was in place, I took the opportunity to invite them to join me for dinner as an expression of my gratitude. They heartily accepted and made the short drive next door while smiling and waving. They thoroughly enjoyed being neighborly, and I was their grateful recipient. Now I was off to the grocery store to stock up on food for myself and pasta ingredients for the dinner I had just planned. But before leaving, I decided to check the answering machine in case the transport service had called.

The only message on my machine was from "Horses Away", the cross-country horse transport service. They'd be here in a few hours. They had had a flat tire on the horse trailer and changing a tire on a fully loaded horse trailer had proved problematical. They assured me that my horses were safe and they apologized for the delay.

It was just as well. I still needed to go to the grocery store and prepare to entertain my neighbors and friends. Additional time was welcome. "Piggly Wiggly." What a name for a grocery store. It had the same small town charm as the store where my mom shopped when I was growing up. And it was small with neatly arranged products on the shelves and polished isles and cashiers in crisply starched uniforms with southern drawls and endearing charm. I gathered a cart full of things and beat a path home to get things unloaded before the horses arrived. I could cook later, before my friends arrived.

This had been a full day, replete with all kinds of work including physical labor, yet I felt invigorated, eager, and hopeful. I had been outside most of the day and I had no quotas or traffic jams or telephone ringing. Things were all falling into place. As I fed the cats, I realized how well they were adjusting to their new home. Exploring all the nooks and crannies of a new dwelling was intriguing to them and I looked forward to letting them outside after we had been here for a few days. Since they had lived their lives thus far in the city, they had been confined to the house. Now that we were no longer city dwellers, I planned to introduce them to the great outdoors. Since I didn't believe in de-clawing cats, they had their defense systems in tact. We were all to be free here in our new home and our new life. Their time would come soon.

The big rig pulled in the driveway at 5:35pm, very late, but very welcomed anyway. Hauling horses across country can take longer than estimated. That is true of the drive without horses, and most reputable haulers drive slower and more carefully when hauling their precious cargo. Becca's horses next door called out a greeting similar to the one I'd received from their humans. The men refused offers for something to drink and set about their task of unloading my two horses that had been strategically loaded last. The slant-load trailer made for a smooth ride and should make unloading easier. Princess Jazmine backed out like a trooper even though her legs were wobbly from the long ride. Her half sister, Zippy never did things the easy way. Instead of backing out like her sister, she went backwards and straight up in the air. She came out of the trailer like a bullet ricocheting off the roof of the trailer. As the blood ran down her face, she shook her head violently. At least she was already out of the trailer. I grabbed my first aid kit and put gauze and pressure on the wound just above her left eye. The gauze was immediately drenched with blood which made me grateful I had already inquired about the vet. Even though the wound wasn't serious, it was big enough and deep enough that it obviously needed stitches. I phoned the vet while the men attempted to keep the horse calm and slow the bleeding.

"I'll be there in ten minutes, Sandy." His voice was reassuring and he had known instantly who and where I was. Thanks again for the grapevine. He arrived in five minutes and I concluded he must not live very far away. He introduced himself briefly to me and then to Zippy before giving her the sedative that would allow him to sew together the edges of the two-inch cut that she had accidentally acquired. She looked like a prizefighter after a rough bout, but she seemed ok. He said he would like to stay to monitor her vitals for a while if I didn't mind. This was a precaution since she'd been shipped and hurt afterwards. I could tell his concern for animals was sincere, and it was apparent that his vet practice was wildly successful. I offered him something to drink, but he declined. We threw some hay to Princess Jazmine, but Zippy was too drugged to eat. Our conversation filled the gaps before he pronounced her safe and drove away. After I paid the bill, he gave me his card and said he would be looking forward to seeing me soon, but hopefully not in an emergency. He said goodbye to Zippy and Princess Jazmine. They liked him and I couldn't help noticing a sly flirtatious smile spread across his face as he waved goodbye to us and said, "Welcome to the neighborhood ladies. Our town is a considerably prettier place now that the three of you are here."

Doc Thompson was a handsome man with a ruddy appearance, tanned skin, dark hair and eyes, and refined features. I heard from Becca later that he'd been married to his high school sweetheart until two years ago when she died of lung cancer. They had two boys he was now raising alone. Becca was exhibiting matchmaking tendencies until I assured her that I had enough changes taking place in my life right now. Finding a mate wasn't on my immediate list of things to do, but he was strikingly good-looking and equally polite. It felt good to have someone flirt with me again. Most importantly, the horse was healing, and both of my girls were in my back yard. Now, I needed to cook dinner.

Pasta is my specialty. Tonight's menu was for
Chicken Asparagus Pasta. I made a penne pasta in a white
crème garlic sauce with sautéed chunks of chicken,
mushrooms, and asparagus topped with mozzarella and
parmesan cheese.

Even though the meal was poultry, I broke with tradition (as
I'm prone to do) and served a California Zinfandel. Tim and
Becca rapped on my door at eight-thirty. I had called to delay
our dinner after the unintended vet visit. Becca had a big
bouquet of fresh-cut flowers in one hand and a book in the
other. She comes bearing gifts. That has become obvious
about her already. Tim's hair was still wet and he looked like
an overgrown kid ready for church. As they stepped through
my doorway, I somehow couldn't imagine that there had been
a time in which they were not my friends. We put the flowers
in water while Tim held the book. Then Becca proclaimed,
"Look, a book about you!" The book was entitled, "Back to
the Beginning", and was about someone else who had decided
to go back to their roots. And I thought my idea was original.

They wanted to see the horses, so we poured ourselves each a
glass of wine and went out to the paddocks. I introduced them
to each one, told them of the bloodlines, and explained the
details of Zippy's accidental bloodletting. They were happy to
hear I agreed with them in my assessment of our local
veterinarian. And I could tell Becca read between the lines in
deducing that I also found Doc Thompson attractive. Since she
seemed to think he walked on water, I wasn't sure who was
being thrown at whom.

We returned to the dining room and ate our fill of the pasta I
had made. They loved my food and I loved my neighbors, my
friends, and my new home.

SEVEN: Significant Meeting

After my neighbors showered me with compliments and left, nature followed suit. That song about rainy nights in Georgia can only be appreciated by a native. When it rains in Georgia it does seem never-ending, yet pleasurably so. As I stood under the overhang of my cabin watching the horses and the rain, I drank in the feelings of home and belonging along with the last of my wine. Lights out here comes with an eagerness to fast forward through sleeping so the next day can unfold. How different this all feels from the Sunday night dread I felt when looking ahead to my workweek in the city. This truly was becoming another life altogether.

Sunlight called me into consciousness as it danced across my closed eyelids. Shorts, flip-flops, and coffee in hand, I made my way to feed the hungry. Cats demand to be first, but now that the horses had joined us, I eventually made my way outside. There is something hypnotic about watching a horse eat. The rhythmic way they lip the hay and finger the grain into their mouths is captivating. I could watch this synergy for hours, but I decided a bigger coffee cup would be in order. After refilling my cup and returning to the horse show in my yard, I noticed that both horses had long and ragged hooves. When horses live in a boarding facility, these aspects of care are arranged by the management without the owner's involvement or awareness. Of course, I paid the bill eventually, but I wasn't involved directly in their care. I had enough responsibility at work. Now I had to find a farrier. I decided to use the more familiar title of "blacksmith" since "farrier" might be a Yankee-sounding word. Heaven forbid. Even though I had grown up in the south, I'd lived on the wrong side of the Mason-Dixon Line for most of my adult life. Another call to Becca yielded a name and phone number to call.

Mackenzie Coleman answered her phone on the third ring and she sounded out of breath. She'd run in from the barn where she'd been doing her morning feeding ritual too. I liked both the sound of her voice as well as her words about her horseshoeing business. We shared the same points of view

about treating horses with respect and gentleness, and
I could tell why Becca liked her so well. She was polite,
friendly, and professional. Her schedule had an unexpected
opening for this afternoon, so we made an appointment for one
o'clock today. She assured me that she always keeps her
appointments as scheduled, and we said our goodbyes. Even
though I had not been directly involved with the farriers in
Ohio, I knew of their reputation for flakiness, so her assurance
was comforting.

Her truck pulled into my driveway at exactly one o'clock. She
was good. As I approached the truck, she stopped, unhooked
her seat belt, and stepped out of the truck. The smile spread
across her tanned face and leaped out at me. She offered her
hand and introduced herself. Her grip was strong from the
work she does. "Mackenzie Coleman…call me Mac. Pleased
to know you Sandy."

"Likewise, I'm sure… and here are the girls. The bay is
Princess Jazmine and the knot head gray is Zippy. She cut her
head making her grand exit from the horse trailer when they
arrived yesterday."

"Wow, Sandy, they're beautiful!" she said with sincerity in
both her voice and her expression. I started into the corral with
my flip-flops from earlier. Mac's look was disapproving and
she was right.

"Sorry for the delay. I shouldda had 'em caught up for you. Be
right back. I need to put on some real shoes, so I don't get to
know the local surgeons right away, too."

When I returned wearing shorts and boots, (very fashionable), I
overheard her talking softly to Princess Jazmine. Her hands
looked tan and strong, yet she caressed the horse with a light
touch and a gentle introductory stroking. Jazmine trusted her
already and so did I.

I haltered Jazmine first and Mac snapped her leather shoeing
apron on and began her work. When she bent over, I couldn't
avoid noticing the tight muscles in her arms and legs. Her job
would do that, since the physical demands must be
extraordinary. That made me wonder what my own backside

must look like after all the years of being sedentary. As she trimmed my horse, she explained what she was doing and why she was doing it. She measured the hooves carefully with an instrument called a hoof gauge. I learned how important balance is to a horse. She used her rasp to round the edges of the hooves. She explained that when she trimmed a horse that was to be left barefoot, she usually included that step. It's called a 'pasture roll' and eases the breakover when a horse takes a step, which also reduces the likelihood of chipping hooves. Her explanations were thorough and useful, and I could tell she loves what she does. Zippy was more of a handful...she usually is. Mac's patience showed through as Zippy yanked her foot away. Instead of losing her temper, she simply picked up the foot again and continued her work. Soon the horse stood blinking sleepy blinks while the back feet were shaped and polished. She looked like she was ready to show…except for that gash over her eye. Mac offered to help me put the medicine on her boo boo and I accepted. Medicating a tall horse with a wounded eye three to four times per day for a few weeks wasn't going to be easy. But it had to be done.

We talked at length about how she got into shoeing horses. She'd been laid off from two different jobs and had decided it was time to choose her own path. I didn't want her to leave, so I was happy when she accepted my offer for a glass of wine. Time to open another bottle. She seemed more like a beer drinker, but said she liked all wine that is not sweet. "This is a treat…easy day and wine afterwards with a new customer. I could be spoiled."

As she washed up in the bathroom, I felt the same way about my day and my life in general. I felt spoiled by myself. My life now revolved around new cool people, my animals, my home, and wine and company. I could easily be spoiled this way as well.

"Corporate life is a distant memory already," I proclaimed, as I popped the cork of an aging Merlot.

"So what did you do in the corporate scheme of things?" she inquired. The smile she arrived with seemed stuck on her face, but the enthusiasm and joi de vivre she exuded were magnetic.

I kicked into gear and told her everything about pagers
and cell phones she ever wanted to know but was afraid to ask.
She said she hated both, but only because she wanted to be free
in the world and unencumbered by phones and other leash-like
devices that yanked her about.

"I know they're popular and some folks need them...especially
city dwellers." She was careful not to offend me. It worked. I
admired her lack of need for the electronic devices that had
represented money in the bank for me for years. We took our
wine outside and sat at the picnic table in the shade. There I
learned about my new farrier. The more she talked, the more I
became aware of her many facets. She was a writer, she liked
to cook, and she raised Golden retriever dogs. She was smart
and articulate and I could tell that her family had been a 'good
one', as they say in the south. Her mother disapproved of what
she was doing for a living. But a southern belle wouldn't
likely look favorably upon getting dirty and working
hard...and sweating your way through life in a trade dominated
by men. It just is not done! We laughed out loud and enjoyed
an easy camaraderie. I almost forgot to pay her for the trims.
We made an appointment for the next trimming in six weeks,
and she wrote down the date and time on one of her business
cards. En route to her truck, she turned towards me and
inquired if I wanted to go riding.

"Absolutely," was my un-thought-out reply. "When?"

"How about this coming Sunday, at nine o'clock in the
morning?" She offered.

"That works for me...my horses or yours?" I asked.

"Let's ride mine this time... give your girls time to adjust and
give Zippy's head time to heal. I'll pick you up since my place
is hard to find. Nine sharp and be ready." Her smile now had
a mischievous quality added. I could hardly wait. Now I had a
new farrier and a riding buddy. What more could I need?
Everyone here was making me feel so welcome. I'd missed
southern hospitality. Now I was drowning in it...happily. And
my life here had only just begun.

In Another Life

"I'll have coffee ready when you get here…you do drink coffee don't you?'

"Oh, hell yeah," came her reply.

"Thank you for trimming my horses, Mackenzie."

"My pleasure, Sandy."

I decided then that not only would she become my pal, but that I wanted to call her Mackenzie instead of Mac. Mac sounded rough and tough, and even though she did the work of a man, she wasn't remotely masculine. She was sensitive and gentle and kind and Mackenzie fit her better. As I affixed her card to the refrigerator door, I was glad we had met. Riding on Sunday would be fun, but I didn't look forward to the sore muscles I knew I would have. At least I'd been riding every now and then in the arena at the boarding facility. Trail riding would be more fun…especially with my new farrier. I didn't have many friends. I guess I had the cut-throat corporate world to thank for that. You trust no one. I did have a few acquaintances back in Ohio. But my career had eclipsed much of a social life. That was my own fault, I suppose.

I was pleased with the few days in my new locale. I was well on my way to establishing myself here. And I'd made several new friends in the process. People here seem eager to embrace a new member of the community. That reminded me of Barb, my best friend from grade school. When she was the 'new kid on the block' in our small town, most people had shunned her. I had thought that to be both limiting and unfair. To me, it was interesting and inviting to have someone new in town. I had asked to sit with her that first day at the school lunch table. We have been friends ever since. Even though we have lived far apart from each other all these years, we have remained close. I value that. Something here gives me that same sense of permanence.

I should call Barb. For some reason, I had not told a great many people about my moving plans. Maybe I didn't want to encounter shock or negativity. It was inevitable that some people might question my actions after years of stability and security. When I make up my mind to do something, I hate hearing quips from people who have no idea what it is like to be me. I really am the only one entitled to my opinion. This may be another way of rationalizing my intrinsic stubbornness. Whatever.

EIGHT: Dating?

The phone startled me out of the book I was reading.

"Hi Sandy, Clayton here, Doc Thompson."

"Hi Doc, Zippy is doing just fine."

"Good hearing that, but I can't claim my only reason for calling is about the horse. I called to ask you to go out to dinner with me. Will you?"

The silence screamed out at me for a response and before I knew it, I'd said, "Yes." It just jumped out of my mouth. But it had come from that place in my mind where I appreciated his looks and that place where I knew we were both single and available. Oh no...a date!

We spoke about Zippy and he said he would pick me up at half past seven. He was relieved to hear I wasn't a vegetarian and told me about the steak house where he planned to make reservations. His flirting had not been my imagination. Before our conversation ended, I'd decided what to wear. The steak house had a western flare so I decided upon jeans and a dress shirt and boots. I was fitting in all right and damn it, I was popular! I wondered aloud if every new woman on the block here is so popular. The spotlight felt warm.

I called Becca and told her about my date. Girl things. She seemed pleased and glad to hear Zippy was healing nicely and that Mackenzie had trimmed both girls.

I told here of our plans to go riding and she assured me that her horses were gentle and we would have fun. There is such comfort in the small circle of neighbors and professionals who all know, respect, and admire each other in a small town. The anonymity of the city was becoming a blur in my memory already.

"Gotta go feed and get ready for my date. Thanks for everything Becca."

"You are very welcome, Sandy."

Clay was right on time. And I was ready. During dinner, we talked about his late wife, his vet practice, and my career and my move. All was typical except for the way he looked at me as if I was a juicy steak. When he was vetting my horse, it was all business. Now it was something altogether different.

"Sandy, I don't mean to be too forward, so forgive me. But you must have sensed that I'm terribly attracted to you?"

"Terribly" was an unusual yet fitting word choice. This was the LAST thing I wanted right now! Right after changing life's gears and moving across country it felt as if this man I'd known for days was about to propose to me. Good grief. Tap the brakes.

"STOP!" was all I could manage to say. But I gestured with both palms outstretched towards his face like blinders. He understood. We ate. Small talk took us to desert. His vet truck with the off–duty vials of medicine clinking around in the back took me home. Nothing more was spoken about his 'attraction.' Goodbye at the door. Home felt safe. He must have felt like an idiot. I thanked him for the dinner on his home answering machine as he drove out of my driveway. Fortunately, the machine allowed me time to explain that I didn't mean to brush off his advances as though insignificant or unflattering. There were just enough changes taking place for me right now and I didn't want the pressure he was about to apply.

"I would like to go out with you again, if you don't hate me", I had said. I hoped this would reassure him and make him feel like less of an idiot. And I did hope he would want to go out with me again. Any matchmaker would call me foolish for not welcoming his advances. I called me honest. I am what I am. Pretenses were left behind in the city…if I ever was saddled with them anywhere. That has never been my style. Not ever.

When the phone rang, I knew he must not live very far away. "I most certainly do NOT hate you, Sandy. I admire your honesty and the fact that you have your own mind. And I will

behave better next time. You call me when you want to try
going out again."

The dial tone revealed his playful side. I liked that. But I still
didn't want to rush to the arms of an obviously horny widower.
And he is my vet. Small town dilemma. I decided to wait a
week or two…or three or four. That way he would know I
really feel the way I profess, yet he wouldn't feel slighted.
And I hoped no horse got hurt in the meantime. You have to
be careful how you step in a small town. Toes are everywhere.

NINE: Riding With Her

The coffee had just finished brewing when Mackenzie's truck became visible in my driveway. Her truck door flew open with abandon and out first came a stunning creature. Mitch, the most handsome Golden retriever dog I'd ever seen. Highlights of auburn glistened in the early day sunlight and I wondered if she'd given him a bath for the occasion. "Howdy, Neighbor," she called out, as she approached my screen door. My new riding buddy sounded like John Wayne only shorter and with a significantly higher-pitched voice.

"Morning! Want some coffee? The pot just finished," I spurted out all at once.

"Thanks, Sandy. Just a little cream, please." With our coffee in hand, we headed for the porch. Lawn chairs, coffee, horses munching hay, and dogs wagging their tails…this is how a Sunday morning should start. Mitch politely introduced himself and then ran after a squirrel around the corner of the cabin. Mackenzie's blue eyes danced to the tune of the adventure our day promised to deliver.

"So, have you always been into horses?" I inquired of her.

"Oh no, I used to be scared to death of them," Mackenzie replied.

She went on to explain that she'd always admired horses yet she was afraid to be near them because of their size and brute force. Even her first few weeks at horseshoeing school had been governed by a powerful reluctance to be underneath the business end of any horse. But how would she make a career of shoeing half-horses? Now her presence among horses and her ease around them showed she'd long since overcome that fear.

"How did you overcome your fear of 'em?"

"Just like anyone else, I guess…I just did it until the fear went elsewhere. Now I'm much more afraid of people!" Her laughter seemed to spill over from a place inside that reacted to all the funny things life had ever sent her way. It got full and she had to laugh a bit in order to make room for more experiences. Frequent laughter is an endearing quality in any human being, especially when it springs from genuine happiness.

"Come on…time to ride out," she proclaimed, as she slammed the coffee cup down on the wooden crate and whistled for Mitch. As she strolled away in the dog's direction, I couldn't help noticing a different spring in her step. This, after all, was her day to play. Since I no longer worked the job of a city drone, I'd forgotten that even country folk are invigorated by time off work. Mackenzie also had on tattered Levi's, which were unlike the crisp new ones she'd worn when working on my horses. And this time she wore a black Stetson hat instead of the baseball cap she'd worn when she was working.

Her hair was long, silky jet black, and always in a ponytail. Even today. Her tattered jeans showed skin in various places that revealed a tan in places most people have none. I looked at her body with admiration and envy…and hope.

Maybe if this riding happens often enough and if I keep bucking my own hay, my body will start to look half that good. One can only hope.

When we made the turn into her driveway, it seemed as if I'd been there already. The pecan tree spread out a protective covering about the entire yard and house. The brick of the house was decorated with ivy that made its way towards the sky. The yard had just been mowed. Fine thing to do on your day off at dawn. I felt important. Horses stood at attention in the pasture that seemed to go on forever. The hillside stretched on into the distance and the fence line was barely visible on the other side of a creek. When her truck stopped one of her horses whinnied. The greeter. They all gathered around her as if she was the pied piper. Only two of them did she halter and bring out to be saddled. One was a small paint named Scout and the other a big chestnut quarter horse named Bubba. She would ride Bubba. Scout was for me. Somehow, I liked riding

the scout horse since I was scouting out the new
territory in an old familiar place. Today would hold more
adventures.

I helped her with the saddles, and within minutes, we were on
our way. Around that same fence now, we picked up the creek
and headed upstream. The water rustled around Scout's legs
but each step he took was sure. Both her horses had shoes on
their front feet. She explained it was for protection and
traction. All seven of her horses have front shoes. That would
have kept her busy.

While we rode, we talked of childhood and how she'd raced
trains on horseback and other things I'd only dreamed of doing.
She seemed so free and seriously busy sucking out all that life
has to offer. Her life reeked of power that would turn a
corporate executive green. Yet she seemed to envy me. My
stories of clutch sales and board meetings and conference calls
seemed to cause her to hang on every word. The horses just
seemed glad to be out and about and stepping in some cool
water.

The grass on the hillside was about knee deep to the horses.
Tempting. But she'd taught them not to graze when under
saddle. After roaming and talking for about an hour and a half,
we stopped and dismounted. The picnic blanket had been
rolled up behind her saddle like a bedroll, and I had not even
recognized it as such. Saddlebags opened and out came
sandwiches and the Colonel's finest fried chicken. Devilled
eggs were her favorite…and we had a dozen to share. They
were a little squashed by the saddlebag trip, but they tasted no
worse for the wear. I liked them the way she'd made them.
Extra mustard seemed to be the ingredient that made hers taste
better. They even had a little paprika atop each one like my
grandmother used when garnishing. The wine, the food, and
the unexpected picnic were perfect. The horses seemed to
think that the grass hit the spot, too.

While we were stopped, she replaced their bridles with halters,
and had hobbled them both. That way they could eat without
running away, which they seemed in no hurry to do. It would
be like our leaving this picnic spread without devouring it all.

That is precisely what we did…right down to the last devilled egg. I can't recall when I'd ever felt so at ease with another human being. My grandmother, maybe.

After we ate, drank, and packed up, we lazily wound our way back over the hills and splashed our way back through the creek to her barn. The old anvil on a tree stump out front and the whisky barrel full of old horseshoes reminded everybody who belonged here. I felt as if I did too.

We unsaddled and hosed off the horses. They were welcomed back into the herd and seemed to relay stories of our outing. Mackenzie offered to show me her house and let me use the restroom before chauffeuring me home. I did both and was aware by her art that she had a fondness for women. This seemed perfectly natural. She was a lesbian. I never would have guessed. I guess I unknowingly had adopted the mental stereotype of the big burley lesbian. This woman wasn't burley or masculine. She was just being herself. That is more than most people can claim. Anyway, I always liked breaking rules, not making them. It had never been my practice to shun people because of their race, sexual orientation, or anything else, for that matter. Especially not people I genuinely liked. Mackenzie was definitely in that category. Her house was tidy, full of pictures and books, and homey. Big couch pillows and ottomans spelled comfort. I hated to leave, but wanted to be back home. My cabin was starting to feel like home already. That house in Columbus, Ohio belonged to other people now…and so did I.

I gave Scout a carrot and thanked him for the ride. Becca had been right about Mackenzie's horses being gentle. As my newfound friend dropped me off at my house, I instinctively hugged her goodbye. She held me with a strong farrier grip and I felt our souls connect.

"I for one am happy you moved here," she stated with sincerity permeating her tone. Her blue eyes were the exclamation point that matched her words. She had no hidden agendas. I like that quality in people, especially since it is so seldom seen.

"Me too." Another profound reply uttered by Sandra Elizabeth Greene. I may not have said anything profound, but the whole day had been remarkable to me. And so was my new farrier who was my new friend, as well.

As I fed my horses and brushed them while they ate, I told them about our ride and about Mackenzie and her horses. Maybe next time we could ride here. Zippy seemed to vote for an outing, but PJ was only interested in one thing. Dinner.

As soon as I sat down inside, the phone rang. It was Mackenzie. "Thank you, Sandy, thank you," was all she said before hanging up.

She was something else. Something true and fresh and alive. I wish she'd given me a chance to reply. That would come soon enough though.

TEN: Local Color

It was Monday morning and I had to go to work. But this work was different. I needed to get my tractor running. If Motorola could only see me now. I called my own personal yellow pages, Becca.

"Mornin' Becca. Wanna come over for lunch…just us gals?" I asked, since I knew it was her day off from the hospital.

She agreed and we set one o'clock as the time. "Want me to bring something?" she inquired.

I said, "No," but knew she would probably would anyway.

"Did you and Mackenzie have fun riding yesterday?" She asked.

"YES, it was great. And we had a picnic and talked about all sorts of things. She's such an interesting person, don't you think?"

"Absolutely, and her horses are a great ride. Didn't I tell you that? Who'd you ride?" she fired double-barreled.

"You were soo right about the horses. I rode Scout."

"WOW, you must rate in her book. He is her favorite and she hardly lets anybody ride him. Glad you had fun."

"Oops, I almost forgot. Who does a woman call to fix her tractor around here? You are my very own talking yellow pages, you know?" I flattered her.

"Bobby Hannah at the John Deere place," she replied without hesitation. "But be careful. He hates his life every day of the week but especially Mondays. Just endure his disposition cause he's not only the best mechanic here…he's the ONLY tractor mechanic in these here parts," she put on an unnecessarily feigned southern accent. Before she hung up, I got the phone number for the dealership. No wonder the old farm tractor I'd inherited was a John Deere. That's all we had in these here parts.

The man who answered the phone must not have been
the acerbic Bobby Hannah. Either that, or Bobby had gotten
the needed personality transplant to which Becca had referred.

"And a GOOD MORNIN' to you this fine day," was how he
answered the phone. "How might Watkins John Deere help
you today?"

"I need to speak to Bobby Hannah?" I stated bravely.

"Just a sec, Ma'am. I'll git him," said Mr. Friendly, whoever.

"Yeah, Bobby," came the proper monotone I expected from
someone who hates his life.

I told him what I needed and he said he would be out to my
place around three...work to do in the shop 'til then. When I
asked if he wanted my name and directions, his reply insulted
me. "You're that city lady trying to make a go here...I know
where your place is," he claimed rudely as he hung up without
a proper goodbye. My years in the business world gave me the
urge to fire the idiot, but then I remembered that he was the
only idiot that could fix my John Deere. And I remembered I
lived in a different world now. You would think that boy's
mama would have taught him how to act. People in the south
are not usually allowed to grow up rude. There must be a story
to go with Mr. Brilliant Mechanic. I wondered how I was
going to deal with him at three o'clock without slapping him or
reminding him of the manners he needed to adopt. I had just
the thing. I would wait until he'd fixed the tractor and give
him a book of etiquette my mama had given me as a child. Just
a subtle hint...AFTER the tractor was fixed. Strategic. In the
meantime, I anticipated a lot of tongue biting on my part. But I
was never known for not speaking my mind, and I didn't intend
on turning over any leaves with respect to that. Not now.

Now that I had a little time on my hands, I decided to go on a
bit of a trail ride. Since the horses were right in my back yard,
I could just saddle up and go. P. J. wouldn't be happy about
leaving her sister behind. But she would just have to deal with
it. I downed another cup of coffee and turned off the pot.
Riding boots slid on much easier than pumps had done for
years past, and I headed out to the horses. When I approached

P.J. with halter in hand, she turned and walked disinterestedly away from me. Oh no. That won't do. I tossed the lead line at her heels. Funny thing about horses: If you want them to come to you, you chase them away. Herding animals see safety in the herd and become fearful when pushed away. I found this amusing and effective. Today, it took three times of systematically walking towards her then chasing her away before she stood still and allowed me to slip the purple halter over her nose. I tied her to a tree and decided I needed a hitching rail. As I brushed the bay horse, I thought of where to put the hitching rail and I thought that this was such a good way to start a day. The hoof pick cleaned a path on each foot. Both saddles were under a tarp on the porch, yet they still had a thick layer of dust on them and the leather was bent in weird directions. I had given strict instructions to the movers about the proper way to transport a saddle. They had obviously ignored me with years of training at disregarding the requests of fussy people who were in the process of moving. In addition to a hitching rail, I decided to build myself two wooden saddle stands…and I would buy real saddle covers to replace the tarp. This was to be a respectable farm, so I would have to dress things up along the way. Once I had my project for tomorrow lined up in my mind, I could then saddle my horse and ride.

I chose the Circle Y saddle. Even under a layer of dust, you could see the quality of the dark brown leather. I tied the familiar girth strap as if I did it every day. Now I just might. Starting my day with a ride would become a ritual. P.J. balked at leaving her sister and Zippy tried to follow. But my spurs goaded her into taking us out of the driveway and onto the dirt road beyond. Zippy's screams could still be heard in the distance, and P.J. took advantage of every opportunity to try to turn for home. My hands grew tired since the muscles for reining a horse were rusty. After an hour or so of this, I was ready to agree with the horse and turn for home.

"O.K. girl, let's go home," I conceded.

Her pace quickened since I accidentally spurred her as her body swung in a tight circle. Plus we were headed home.

Horses show new life on the way home. Now I had to constantly slow her progress like a car that had begun to idle too high. Riding the brakes is not good for a car. Neither is getting into a horse's mouth this much. I chose to turn her in a few tight circles just to halt her forward progress. She got very agitated when I kept doing those circles. I decided at that moment that I needed a horse trainer. Partly for me to learn how to deal with these things and partly for my horses to learn this new life. They were used to an arena and barns where they were always together. Trail riding had to be better if you are a horse, even though this meant being left behind from time to time. AND maybe somebody else could join me for my morning rides so both horses could go out. Mackenzie! I wondered expectantly if she would wanna do that. Tonight I would call and ask. The worst she could do was say no.

Zippy seemed relieved she'd not been left alone forever. My weary hands undid everything and brushed the saddle imprint from P.J.'s fur. The limp carrot in my pocket made it all worthwhile for P.J. and after picking her feet out again, I returned her to her corral. I thought to call Mackenzie right away while the idea was fresh.

"Hi Mackenzie, this is Sandy," I said to her answering machine. "I have a problem with my horses. Could you call me as soon as possible?" In sales, we are taught how to get a response and I had instinctively planted an idea in her head.

Within minutes, she called back. She'd been on her way in when she heard my message.

Concern punctuated her voice, "Got your message. Everybody ok?"

"Yeah, I didn't mean to scare you," I apologized and continued, "I just wanted to know if our riding buddy relationship could become a daily thing?"

"Everyday? You expect me to start every day going on a ride with you?" she asked.

I was starting to feel silly and guilty for asking when she blurted out her characteristic, "Oh, Hell Yeah! When does this deal start, tomorrow?"

My smile now matched the one in her voice. I explained how my ride went and how Zippy acted and all that. She understood and declared that we needed to ride my horses for a few months straight but that we should give Zippy's eye a chance to heal first. "It really is unfair to ride an injured horse, don't you think?" she asked.

"Absolutely," I agreed. I liked that about her. I'd seen people at my former boarding facility ride their horses when they were limping or wounded somehow. People do not relish physical activity when wounded, and I never understood doing that to a horse. But most people are just not that sensitive.

"Just short rides, though… and at a walk, maybe," she requested. "My job is physical and I can't afford to wear myself out before my work day starts," she explained.

"Of course," I empathized. "I do not, for the life of me know how you can do that kind of work every day, as it is. I'll be considerate." We made a plan and I hung up. I could hardly wait until eight o'clock in the morning. What a twist. I used to dread the traffic, the pantyhose, and all those things about starting a new day. Now I would start each day on the back of a horse…except Sundays. Mackenzie had to have a day to sleep in. She took Sundays and Mondays off and needed one day to sleep late if she could.

Becca was right on time at one o'clock and our chicken salad sandwiches hit the spot. Riding and working outdoors perks up a woman's appetite. In the city, I skipped a lot of meals unless I needed to meet with a client. Now I found myself eagerly gobbling up life and the food that gave me energy. The banana bread Becca had made this morning was a perfect dessert. She listened intently as I told her about Bobby's rudeness and my plans to slip him a book on manners as well as my riding outing and plans to ride every day with Mackenzie. Tim might get laid off from his job and they were worried about making ends meet if he did.

"How can they lay off firefighters? Don't we always need them?" I questioned.

"You would think so, but the last levy failed and funds are low. He has lotta years in, so he might not get cut. That's what we're counting on," she replied with trained optimism.

Before I knew it, the work truck barreled down the driveway. Out popped Bobby Hanna with all the enthusiasm of the cork from a bottle of flat champagne. Not only did he know who I was and where my farm was, but also he knew where the old John Deere had died. I doubt this had anything to do with North Star guidance.

Becca thanked me for the lunch and headed home. She was in no mood to deal with "Personality Embodied." By the time I reached Bobby, he already had the hood open and had hooked a battery tester to the tractor. The needle on the tester was non-responsive. So was Bobby. No great mystery or surprise on either count. The tractor had died in place over twenty years ago with the bush-hog still attached and useless. I wondered if I was going to have to buy a new tractor and make a giant planter out of this one.

Bobby worked without a word. Engines were his specialty…not people. He removed the old battery, installed the new battery, and tried the engine. No luck. Systematically he checked the gas tank. Must have been enough gas in the tank, because he replaced the cap and proceeded to remove something else. My guess was the starter. After replacing it, the old tractor started with the first turn of the key. He WAS good. That cocky know-it-all look was back on his face. But the tractor was running for the first time in twenty years. There was grass flying from the bush-hog and some liquid flying from the engine. He disengaged the attachment and peered into the engine despite the liquid that was now drenching his green and white uniform. He looked, he sniffed, and he shut her off.

His truck had an assortment of spare parts ready for this occasion and after fitting and replacing several hoses, changing the oil and filter, lubricating all the fittings, topping off all the

40

fluids, he started her up again. He adjusted his John Deere cap and spit out the juice from the big wad of chewing tobacco that pooched out his left cheek. How attractive. But off he went like the wind…bouncing up and down and turning circles as he went. He was looking and listening all the way. He engaged the bush-hog and cut a swath with it that left him satisfied. It left me with the rest to mow. As soon as the engine shut down, he put on the brake and went to work with the wrench that he pulled from his back pocket. He then appeared to go through a checklist in his mind. The hood slammed shut and he looked at his wristwatch on his way to the truck. He'd not said a word to me so far and I was afraid he would leave without my opportunity to enlighten him about the manners he needed to employ. But as I looked at my watch, I decided not to do that, after all. Bobby had only been at my farm for an hour and forty-two minutes. And my tractor was running like a deer. Ha ha.

The grease-splotched bill he handed me stopped my laughter in its tracks. But since it was infinitely cheaper than a new tractor, I paid it without whining. He still had not spoken a word to me. Charm wasn't his forte. He hung his head like he was ashamed of himself or ashamed of his life. He got in the truck, shut the door, and spoke. "Thank ya, now. Lemme know when somephin else breaks," he muttered without looking up from under that greasy green hat. "And call Dusty over there at Georgia Tire…you need new tires if you figure out how to use this thang…them's rotted and gonna bust. Dusty…He's in the book."

There was so much I wanted to say but instead of saying anything I'd planned or doing all that I had planned to do, I simply folded the receipt and put it in the etiquette book I still clutched under one arm. So much for remedial manners. But my tractor worked.

That little dig had really gotten under my skin. I'd bitten my tongue, but I'd not forgotten it. Just because I'm a woman, Bobby had assumed that I obviously knew nothing about running a tractor or bush hog. I'd show him. I put down the book on the porch and donned my grandpa's straw fishing hat.

41

It could double as a lawn-mowing hat. Clean swaths
around my cabin looked good. And it was fun to step on one
brake and feel the tractor turn a tight circle underneath me.
This would have been fun to have in rush hour traffic. As I
passed by the horses, they bucked and ran in their corrals. The
noise of the motor revved them up as well, it seemed, but I was
careful not to get too close. Rocks fly.

With the yard all mowed I decided to both park and name my
mower. 'Buford' seemed like a good name for a tractor. And I
decided to park it near where the barn would eventually be. I
tilted the seat up in case of rain just like my granddaddy used
to do. My sweat now replaced his on the brim of his old straw
hat. And I felt good about my day. The horses gobbled up
their hay and grain.

Before I went in to fix myself dinner, I dusted off the other
saddle. It was a black cordura nylon Big Horn…lighter than
my big Circle Y. I would use that one on P.J. in the future and
Mackenzie would get the Circle Y. She wanted to ride Zippy
when we started riding my horses. Anyone who saw her move
wanted to ride her. She floated over the ground like a graceful
bird. I had not ridden many horses in my lifetime, but she was,
without a doubt, the smoothest horse I'd ever encountered.

I doctored Zippy's eye and went inside. My cabin looked good
with horses foraging about and a freshly mown yard. I hoped it
wouldn't hurt the tractor to mow with the "rotted" tires. That
reminded me to call the tire place. "Dusty, proper name for a
fella runnin' a tire place," I muttered to myself as I dialed the
number from the phone book. In my mind's eye, I could see
the tire place. My granddaddy had held my hand there once
when I was a child and he let me watch them fix our flat tire.
He explained all the steps and what the weird machine was
doing as it stripped the tire from the rim. Finding the hole
using soapy water and bubbles had intrigued me, and I missed
Granddaddy. They could come out two days from now and
replace all four tires. The estimate nearly knocked me off my
feet. But a thousand dollars for tires coupled with the amount
of Bobby's bill was a mere drop in the bucket compared to the
price of an entire tractor. Little had I known that my profit

sharing would come in handy on a farm. City life had been so different. And less of an accomplishment, it seemed. Even though I'd brokered deals in the hundreds of thousands of dollars, this somehow seemed more monumental. It was something for me...for my farm...for my home.

I wanted this day to end and the morning to hurry and arrive so I could go riding again. So I could be around Mackenzie again. So I could drink in more of this new life again. It would come in due time.

ELEVEN: Bonding

The day did arrive. And so did my new riding buddy.

"How the hell are you?" She asked with a smile as wide as her face. There is something special about the way a friend greets another friend. Even though we had not known each other long, Mackenzie greeted me like we were old chums.

"Fine as frog hair," I chirped back. My new friend doubled over with laughter. She'd honestly never heard that saying.

"Do frogs even have hair?" she quizzed.

"Yep…just goes to show you how fine it is!" I proclaimed, as we laughed in sync.

"So, city girl…you sore?" she teased.

"Of course," I confessed. "But more riding is the best cure for that."

"Good thinking," she praised me as she reached for the coffee cup I offered.

"Mmm," she purred after slurping the warm brew. "Nothing quite like that first sip of coffee in the morning, eh?"

"You know, I could have driven to your place today…now that I know where you are," I said apologetically.

"But then I would miss out on this coffee…mine is not remotely this good," she said with emphasized sincerity. "Tomorrow you can drive yourself over if you disclose your coffee source. We sound like a commercial…where are the hidden cameras? And do NOT try and tell me you have secretly replace this with decaf, 'cause I'll leave right now!" she exclaimed.

"It's organic espresso blend. They sell it in stores here. I'll bring you some," I promised. "My gift to my new riding buddy."

"This deal gets better all along, Sandy. I have really missed riding, too." She went on to explain that she used to ride all the time with a girlfriend…not a "girlfriend" in that sense of the

44

word. They had ridden almost every day, as we had begun doing, but her friend's controlling lover had gotten jealous and reined in her woman. I knew men who had done that with my friends. I guess it really is no surprise to learn that women who are romantically involved would encounter the same snares.

"We are not even friends any more thanks to the evil girlfriend...but that was her goal all along, I think."

"I never will understand controlling people," I mused, as I sipped from my coffee, too. "Or why people allow themselves to be controlled."

"Never worked for me," Mackenzie stated succinctly. "You ever been married?" she added.

"Unfortunately, yes. Happily divorced, thank you very much," I announced as we both laughed in unison again.

"Somehow, I can't picture you in an unhappy marriage," she rolled her eyes as if she were trying to envision events being projected onto my ceiling.

"Me either...now," I professed. "But I have the pictures to prove it. Somewhere in a box around here," I said as I searched with my eyes from box to box.

"Later," she commanded as she pulled me towards the door. "Right now, we have horses to ride!" I turned off the coffee maker and the light, grabbed my scrunchy brown cowboy hat, and locked the door. We had not even started our ride yet, but I was really enjoying myself already. Sometimes you meet people in this life who you knew already. That is how I was beginning to feel about Mackenzie. An easiness. A level of comfort that you may never achieve with some people was present already with Mackenzie.

I watched her walk towards her truck and felt the magnetism she exuded. We chatted about her evening, my yard mowing, and mine. When we arrived at her barn I realized she wasn't kidding when she'd said we had horses waiting.

"You already pulled 'em out?" I inquired.

"Yes, Maham," she drawled. "Mackenzie Coleman, at your service."

"I'm sorry," I frowned and said. The horses had been tied up the whole time we were lazily slurping our morning coffee.

"Do not be sorry," she admonished. "It's all training! And all trail horses need to know how to stand tied."

"Oh, goodie. Now you're divulging trade secrets," I squealed. "Part of the reason your horses are so well trained."

"I learned well in the School of Hard Knocks," she revealed.

"Me too," I followed. "Speaking of my marriage. Wanna hear all the ugly details?"

"Yeah, and I do want to see those pictures after our ride," she reminded me. "You do know this is my day off, don't you?"

"I'd forgotten." It would be great to visit more later. As with any close friend, I never seemed to tire of her company, conversation, and enthusiasm for life itself.

"More coffee, too," she added.

"Of course!" I promised.

We rode for over an hour at a slow lazy saunter almost. The horses seemed to enjoy our meandering around and they even seemed to be listening to all the unhappy details of the dregs of my bad marriage. So did Mackenzie. But there were funny parts…surprising as that may seem. The funniest was the part about how my ex-husband had made an issue in open court about the strain I'd placed on him by wanting to have sex too often!

"Now that has got to be a first…for a man to complain about that," she laughed and shook her head.

I explained the laughter of all the participants in the courthouse that day…even the stenographer had laughed as she typed on her little machine. It was funny, but the pain of it all surfaced in my mind at the same time. My ex must be part of a select few men who saw sex as a chore. Even in almost a decade of marriage, we had never shared that closeness that can be achieved sexually. Even though I gave my new friend an overview of the whole failed marriage, I didn't reveal my wounded spirit. But she guessed it.

"That must have hurt," she said with feeling, as she looked right into my eyes softly.

I looked away, and tried to forget those feelings of hurt and shame. Shame I'd felt just by being normal and healthy and sexual. I am after all very sexual. Always have been.

"Yeah...but that is all behind me, now," I proclaimed like the survivor I'd become during that decade of my life. And I changed the subject to happier things.

"Tell me some farrier adventures...I'm sure you have stories to tell," I demanded.

"Boy, howdy, do I!" she admitted. "Where shall I begin?"

So we rode and laughed as she told about adventures in horseshoeing. During all those years while I was slaving away in the city and on the freeway, she was handling crises of her own in a very different world. And she was having fun doing it every day. Even her routine days sounded exciting to me because they were so different from mine. Now they were meshing.

We wound our way back home...to Mackenzie's home. Then we unsaddled and brushed out the horses. To me it is a crime to leave a horse 'ridden hard and put away wet.' So we brushed both of her horses thoroughly and turned them out to rejoin their herd. They ran and squealed at each other and proceeded to roll in the dirt. The ones that had been left behind seemed to fuss at Scout and Bubba as if they were school children that had suddenly become the teacher's pets.

En route to Mackenzie's truck I realized just how sore my neophyte muscles had become. And my arms were sore from steering Buford. Tractors have a lot of things, but mine definitely didn't have power steering.

"City girl," I harrumphed. "How long you gonna call me that?"

"As long as it fits," she teased. She was being playful again. She liked that. But so did I. Banter friends. There is a comfort in that. Someone once said, "I only tease people I really like." This was that. Some teasing is mean-spirited. This wasn't. And after all, I was a city girl…or at least I had been for a very long time. But times they were a changing. I wondered if Bobby Hannah had seen my freshly mown yard, yet. Not bad for a girl…and a city girl, to boot.

We returned to my cabin and I made a fresh pot of organic coffee.

"What's special about organic coffee?" Mackenzie asked, as she read the label on the can I'd just opened.

"No pesticides," I explained. "Most coffee is loaded with pesticides unless it is grown organically."

"Who knew?" She said with a glimmer.

I went on to explain that pesticides interfere with hormone balance and that years of drinking non-organic coffee had gotten me all out of whack.

"Must've been what made you so horny…..too bad for your poor husband."

"Very funny….and there are many other reasons he is my EX-husband, remember?"

"Sorry," she seemed sincere. "Good to know about the coffee though…good to learn something from the city girl." That smile stretched playfully across her face again.

"Let's see them pictures, now, "City Girl," she requested, using improper grammar on purpose.

I motioned for her to follow me into the den and found the old hat box that housed my photos. For some reason all of us seem to store the majority of our photographs in an old box of some sort. Photo albums seem neglected. But not the boxes. And only I knew who all these people were and the significance they each held. After shuffling through the stack of photographs, I separated out the wedding photos as well as the other 'family' photos of the ex and me.

"Oh, my God!" she gasped, "You look so sad."

"I was sad…profoundly sad," I remembered aloud.

Mackenzie studied each photo I handed her…. the engagement picture from the newspaper, the one of me in my satin wedding gown, and the ex and me with our carved pumpkins at Halloween. She seemed to be searching with her eyes to find the hidden emotions. Like finding the hidden pictures in those magazines we loved as children. She had pinpointed the main one already.

"You were pretty then too, though," she declared boldly, even though she didn't look up when she said the words.

"Thank you," I replied, as I hid my flushed face by turning towards the kitchen to retrieve the coffee pot. I plopped the pot and the creamers in a tray nearby while we sifted through each one of those old photographs. There was one of my trip to Williamsburg, Virginia as a child. I had on a soldier's helmet. Another was me standing in front of the house where they filmed the Beverly Hillbillies television show in California. 'My Life in Pictures,' by Sandra Elizabeth Greene. No one had ever looked through all these pictures except me. Mackenzie seemed genuinely interested in knowing all about the details of each vacation, each amusement park, each horse, and each house. My house that was no longer my house. She noticed the tear. And she hugged me amidst all the photographs on the floor of my new home.

"It'll be o.k." she promised. "You'll be happier here."

I felt silly crying over the house I'd sold. After all it was my idea. Already, in just a few days, I'd rekindled all the cozy feelings of home that this cabin evoked long before my recent arrival.

"Here's me and my granddaddy at this very cabin!" I announced, as I plucked a Polaroid from the pile like a card drawn knowingly from the deck. "We had been fishing…see?"

"Good catch," she observed. "Bream?" She asked, in reference to the string of fish I was holding in the picture?

"Yep…and boy did they taste good that night for dinner," I said longingly. I sure did miss fishing with my granddaddy. And I missed the way my grandmamma fried them to a perfect golden brown complete with hushpuppies.

"Let's go fishin', "City Girl!" Mackenzie exclaimed with all the wonderment of a small child. But I was rapidly tiring of my new nickname.

"How long you gonna call me that?" I asked with unmasked disapproval.

"I already told you how long," she replied. But I think she was catching on.

"Does that mean you're gonna call me that exclusively, now?" I tensed.

"O.K.," she conceded. "Didn't mean to ruffle your feathers."

"Accepted…and yes, I can't wait to go fishing," I answered with a smile.

"Well I just so happen to know a woman who has a pond…been stocked for years," she revealed as she eyed my pond through the open window.

We had such a good time. For hours we drank strong coffee and identified each and every photograph in my collection. It meant so much to have someone show such an interest in these snapshots. Glimpses into my life. Now I didn't even mind the fact that I'd not gotten around to organizing them into a photo album like a real person. My cabin had always been a happy place full of good memories and family. This afternoon with my new pal only added another patch to that quilt of warm memories.

TWELVE: Exploring

Time seemed to roll lazily along here. The days seemed to all escape me, yet they left me filled with a new sense of wonder. And of home. Even though I lived alone, I definitely had a home life. Most days started with a trail ride. Zippy's eye healed in no time at all, and she'd become Mackenzie's mount. It made me more than a little jealous to see the way my horse looked at my farrier and my friend. But I was glad the horse was getting to do things. I'd always promised her a fun life. Since I was having fun, I assumed she was, as well. We were all getting fit. Sore muscles were a thing of the past. Thank God.

One day in particular, I had been quite the carpenter. I'd built myself two very lovely hitching rails. Four by four posts sunk two feet into the ground. They were fettered in place by a bag of concrete in each hole. For some reason, I adored setting things in concrete. There's something about the chemical reaction and the permanence of it all. I hoped to myself that they were sturdy enough since both of my horses had been known to pull back. Those horses in the Western movies don't ever move a muscle when their rider dismounts to go into the saloon. Mine would be in the next zip code if I ever just flipped the reins over the railing like they do in those movies. Another shining example of the fact that life just ain't like the movies.

I had intended to build the saddle racks, but that would have to wait for another day. Life had fallen out of this day. I captured a photo of my completed project. My friends in the city would admire my handiwork. Boy was my life different than theirs, and I was glad. But I was famished and exhausted, as well.

It was after nine o'clock when the phone awakened me. I'd been napping in my recliner after supper. It was Clayton, my vet, and not-so-secret admirer.

"Wanna try again?" He asked.

"Whatever happened to me calling you when I was ready?" I asked.

"I thought you never would," He admitted. "There's this Chinese place here…you'll like the food…"

"Promise to behave?"

"Promise. Pick you up at eight tomorrow night?" he asked almost begging. But he was trying very hard. And he was disarmingly handsome.

I agreed. Sleep rolled over me. The cats had curled all around me as if we were going to spend the whole night in that chair. Not so. I flipped off all the lights and flopped deep into my welcoming bed. I was going riding in the morning. Had to sleep fast and get it out of the way.

My alarm rang and my feet eagerly greeted the floor. Jeans, coffee started, and horses fed. It was only six o'clock, but I'd gotten accustomed to feeding early so they could have a snack before our ride. And I wanted to shower before going. I felt a bit silly doing that, but I'd fallen asleep in my chair after dinner and never bathed after my day of riding and mowing and carpentering.

"Mornin' You!" Was her greeting this day. The smile on her face made me smile, too. That was how she was. I opened the screen door and handed her the coffee mug on the way in…the one with the two horses on it. That seemed right for her. We drank one cup inside and another on the porch. A soft breeze fluttered and flirted with us to be on our way. I showed her my hitching rails and told her about my date with Clay tonight.

"Aha," she said, as she admired my handiwork. "Might very well be time for a new nickname for you, now."

"Didn't know I could build things, huh?" I bragged. I really was pleased with myself. "I'm gonna build some saddle racks, too."

"Let's see if these hitchin' rails hold up," she said, poking fun at me as she caught up 'her' horse.

We saddled up and rode out. Mackenzie was an inch or two taller than me, and when she sat atop the taller horse, I had to really look up to her. We rode right through the river and

Mackenzie stopped Zippy midstream. Reins in hand, she jumped down. The water was up to her waist, but instead of minding, she took off her hat and dove under. Zippy pawed at the water and tried to follow suit. As quickly as she'd dismounted, she swung herself back up effortlessly. Water cascaded downward across the saddle and the horse, and back toward its origin.

"Go ahead! Your turn," she dared me with a wave of her hand as an invitation to dive in.

"I already had my shower today," I said, but before I knew what I was doing, I found myself underwater. My horse lay down and started to roll, saddle and all. I have no idea how she did it so fast, but Mackenzie jumped off of Zippy and grabbed the slippery reins from my hands. She was pulling the horse to her feet as I was emerging from the water.

"We better get these two out of here while we still can," her eyes laughed, yet her voice sounded urgent. Dripping on the bank, we laughed at ourselves and the horses shook more water on us both.

"Are we going to add this to our routine every day, too?" I asked about the impromptu swim, as I sputtered water off of my face.

"You just never really know. Maybe we should," she said playfully. "Race you to that tree," she challenged as she swung back up on Zippy's back and took off.

P.J. had to run faster since her little legs were shorter. Plus, with their head start, we had little or no chance. I was just lucky to have gotten on before my horse darted. This was fun. I felt like a kid out playing with my pals. Who said being in your forties had to be boring? Somebody had obviously forgotten to tell Mackenzie all the rules about growing older. We were both out of breath when we got to the tree. So were our horses.

"You must've changed your mind about that only walking part," I reminded her of her admonition about her physical job and all.

"Exceptions to every rule," she confessed with a grin.

While we leaned on the tree, I noticed that my right stirrup was missing. In all the excitement, I'd not even felt it fall. We retraced our steps on foot and found it floating in the river like a strange sort of catamaran without a sail.

"Get back on, please," she instructed, "I'll adjust it for you."

As I sat in the saddle she held my leg in place and I studied her face. Water beaded on her seal-black hair that now fell all around her shoulders. No ponytail. As she carefully fastened my stirrup back on the saddle, my eyes followed the trail of water as it dripped off her hair and her nose and her lips. Down her neck and into her shirt it went. She wasn't wearing a bra…and I found myself staring. The wet tank top clung to her muscled yet obviously female form. She sensed that my eyes were following the water. This was uncharted territory for me. She continued tethering the stirrup back into place.

When I took off her hat with one hand and traced the water as it ran down the side of her face and down her neck with my other hand, she stopped looking at the stirrup. Her left eyebrow dipped up, as if to ask what was happening. Her eyes looked expectant and inviting. So I did it again. Softly I caressed her face, much like a blind person might do to learn a person's face. But I wasn't blind. And this was a woman I found myself caressing. Her face felt strong and kind and soft beneath my exploring fingertips. The look in her eyes spoke volumes. At least a minute, maybe more passed by without a word. Both our eyes darted, both our hearts danced…at least mine did. My face flushed, but I wasn't the least bit hesitant or uncomfortable. Neither was Mackenzie. It was a moment frozen in time, and frozen in a memory…just like the snapshots we had investigated on my living room floor. Only profoundly different.

After she seemed certain I was finished tracing her silhouette, she yanked on my stirrup and helped me replace my foot.

"You're all set now, my dear," she said, with a new affection I noticed and liked. Mackenzie had become dear to me. All those hours of riding horses, disclosing information about our families and our dreams and disappointments. She'd slowly and steadily become such a part of my heart. Good relationships evolve unhampered and without effort, just because. And most of the time, you can't even remember what it was like before someone became so important that when you think to yourself, it's as if you are talking aloud to them.

"Thanks, Country Girl," I played. And I returned her hat.

"Thank You!" she said, and I knew what she meant. She never took her blue eyes off mine as she walked around my horse to get to hers. Zippy must have sensed our moment because, not only did she not run off, but also she had not tried to roll in the water either. Good girls.

For what seemed like an eternity, we rode in silence. Her strong upright frame looked good on my horse. We had turned toward home and both horses quickened their pace. P.J. tossed her head to let me know that she wanted to lead. As I passed her I could feel Mackenzie's eyes. I could almost sense her thoughts, too. It felt so right to have touched her face. All of this felt right.

We rode the rest of the way home easily and without a word. I suppose we were both remembering. I was. When we got back to my house, we hitched the horses to the rail, unsaddled, and brushed them down. She got new carrots from the front seat of her truck. The girls eagerly ate the whole package. We hugged goodbye and she kissed me tenderly on my neck. A short puff of air escaped me in response.

"Have fun on your date tonight," she said playfully over her shoulder as she turned to leave.

"Oh no, I forgot about that!" I admitted.

"Somethin' on your mind?" was her way of asking if I was all right.

"Yeah," I declared proudly. "Something wonderful." The look in her azure eyes told me this pleased me. She looked right through me with those eyes that continued to talk to me long after she'd driven out of sight.

I followed the progress of her truck as she drove away.
But I stood there for a long time deep in thought. Then I sat
down on my porch. I propped my feet up and I closed my
eyes. And I traced her face again in my mind. All the while I
was exploring the possibilities.

Clayton, my date, was right on time. The food was luscious,
and the good vet did behave himself. Thank God. I told him
about my tractor repair and the hitching rails I'd built. Riding
horses with Mackenzie had become an integral part of my
days. He smiled at our adventures and agreed that it sounded
like we were having fun. I left out the most important part.
But that was none of his business.

I was glad that our previous date had ended so abruptly
because he'd been too forward. That insured that he wouldn't
dare to attempt a kiss. As the door closed behind him, my eyes
closed. But Clayton Thompson was the furthest thing from my
mind. Sleep came easily after a day that was full. But that
seemed to be the case these days, since all of my life was full
and physical. I drank in the fresh air and the sunshine and all
the Georgia things.

As I slept that night I dreamed that my grandparents were still
alive. They were here, at my cabin. Their cabin. The four of
us were fishing in our pond…. Granddaddy, Grandmamma,
Mackenzie, and me. We were all catching fish in rapid-fire
succession and we scaled them afterwards on the back porch.
Then my grandmamma fried them up. We ate and drank dark
beer in frosty mugs. Except for my grandmamma…. she was
never much of a beer drinker. When I awoke, it was
disappointing to realize they were not still here. And I wished
they could have met Mackenzie in real life. Maybe that was
their way of saying they had.

THIRTEEN: Farming 101

Weeks passed. Weeks of "work". Somehow farming does not sound like work…but it definitely is. My John Deere tractor did the real work, but I was the farmer. Part of the reason I'd chosen to move here was so that I could grow my own crops. Organic vegetables.

So, after hours of reading on the subject, I started out preparing the soil. I measured and staked off where the corn would go... the zipper peas, the okra, and all the rest. Ball mason jars stood empty in my cupboards, but I intended to change that. Soil ripped behind me like an open wound as the tractor chugged forward. In my Granddaddy's fishing hat, I looked the part. The corn would be first. After readying the earth, I threw the kernels to their fate in neat rows. Using the box blade, I covered up my vegetable-to-be and watered. For now, I'd strategically placed sprinklers. Eventually, I would find out how to install some sort of irrigation tubing. This was a start.

My horses watched. The first thing in the mind of every horse drawing breath is "FOOD?" Little did they know that this was indeed to yield food. But not food for them. My plan was to grow most of what I liked to eat. Instead of going to the grocery store, I would go to my cellar to shop. Self-sufficiency appealed to me. So did the idea that I knew that no noxious chemicals had been pumped into my soil before the seeds were left to germinate. No pesticides would coat the leaves of my crops, either. Ever. For years in Ohio I have said that "No-till farming" was going to kill us all. No more. Why would anyone want to eat food that had been grown in poison? But organic food is so hard to come by because so few people understand what it even is. I would have to use something to combat the bugs. Research would enable me to find a biodegradable and non-toxic way to prevent the inevitable damage of pests. Research was something I'd done for years. But this was more personal.

I guess I was engrossed in setting the little flags in place. Flags to mark where the rows of corn were planted. Mackenzie's truck was parked behind my Trooper.

"Nope," She said first and startled me as she spoke.
"No City Girl any more," she said as she looked over my corn-field-in progress. Then she looked me over, as well.

"I look the part, though, don't I?" I asked.

"Got any sweet tea, my dear?" she invited.

"I sure do," was my reply, "I could use a glass, myself." I was so glad to see her unexpectedly.

"To what do I owe the surprise visit?" I asked.

"Problem with a customer," she frowned. "I could use some advice from a shrewd business woman I know."

"Yeah, I definitely look like a shrewd business woman right now," I said as we laughed together. We did that a great deal whenever we were together. That was one of the ever increasing reasons I found I liked the company of this woman.

"Let's sit out here," I motioned to the porch as I set down the pitcher of sweet tea. Mackenzie had brought our tumblers out with her when she realized we were taking our tea party outdoors. We both downed an entire glass in unison.

"You worked up a thirst out here plowing, Sally Field?" She asked with a grin.

"Huh?" I expressed my lack of understanding with my trademark eloquence.

"Remember the movie "Country" with Sally Field playing a farmer woman?" She asked playfully.

"O.K., I get it…. and yes, planting my corn crop did work up a thirst, thank you," I added.

As she relayed the story of her problem customer, I listened carefully. Her eyebrows furrowed as she spoke, and I could sense the passion she felt for her business. People tend to take advantage of her because she is kind-hearted and easy going. The sun flirted with the clouds as we had our business meeting on the porch. My advice was welcomed. Unlike many other of my business meetings.

In Another Life

After draining the whole pitcher of tea, we both had to use the bathroom. I allowed my guest to go first and then I did so hurriedly. We walked back onto the porch…talking as we went. Mackenzie turned her head craning her neck toward the new pitcher of sweet tea on the picnic table. And I did it again. Traced her face. Down her neck and up again. I'd wanted to…wanted to do that again. She froze and stopped talking.

She looked down at the glass the whole time. Soft sweet skin beneath my fingers. No rough man face with razor stubble. Strong cheekbones, yes. But soft, not tough. And kind. She gracefully lifted her chin and turned to face me. Her soft blue eyes met mine. They said, "Go ahead." I paused for some reason. But our eyes didn't. I studied her sweet face. She studied mine. Of all the words we had shared over the time we had known each other, these unspoken ones were the most profound and meaningful.

Then I used my other hand…like the mate joining a set of living bookends. I traced both sides of her face with both of my hands. Gently, I turned her face towards mine. Carefully and with purpose, I found her lips with mine. My eyes were closed, but I could still see hers. They were indeed soft. But they were hungry. I carefully cradled her face in my hands, and her hands found my face deliberately. She breathed out fast…little spurts that revealed nerves. But my heart was racing, as it had not done in years. She sweetly kissed back…letting me lead. I was the one who started this, and I could tell she wanted more. But she was careful not to misstep.

She let out a little grunt of pleasure when I ran my tongue between her teeth and into her welcoming mouth. Exhaling hard, she followed my lead. She spread out her hand on the left side of my face as we kissed. Nobody had ever touched my face like that. Ever.

Her hands felt strong yet gentle as they moved across my skin. The work she did made her skin rough. But she wasn't remotely too rough. She caressed me and she kissed me and I could feel myself melting. Being caressed by a woman was entirely different…and entirely wonderful. She was so strong and soft all at the same time. I kissed her for as long as I dared.

59

She kissed back hungrily, slowly, tenderly, carefully, and with understanding in her tongue.

When I stopped, our eyes opened and met up again. We picked up the conversation at a glance. Up close. Then she took the lead. Oh how wonderful it felt. She pulled me close so she could reach my mouth again. Muscles strained beneath her shirt. My farming hat fell to the porch. I wouldn't dare reach for it. Not now. Her long urgent kiss told me she wanted more and so did her tight nipple as it brushed my shoulder. No bra again. While we kissed, I concentrated on telling her everything I could with my tongue and my mouth and my hands. And I wondered why this didn't feel unnatural at all. At this point, I could care less about convention.

All this on my front porch. In front of God and everybody. In the heart of the Bible belt. But I didn't care. I really didn't. All I cared about was kissing her for as long as she would let me. And she wasn't only letting me. Now she was kissing me. Willing prisoner in her strong arms. Nothing can compare to that first kiss. Every intimate detail of it is etched in my senses. My whole body poised. Waiting. Wanting more. When she finally slowed to a stop, kissed deliberately, briefly on my wet lips, and pulled back, I smiled. She wasn't sure. That's why I smiled. It helped.

"I thought you were never going to do that," she confessed.

"I didn't exactly plan to," I admitted. "But sometimes things don't go according to plans."

"Could I have a drink…a real drink, after that?" she asked.

"Yeah, if I can have another kiss," I flirted unabashedly. And I thought I'd forgotten how.

"You bet," she said as she smiled and gingerly reached for my mouth.

Oh, God, how I ached to kiss this woman! And it didn't even feel weird. But I had never been one to follow convention. After all, people who have a comfortable house and a safe and lucrative career are not supposed to quit. As John Cougar Mellencamp said in a song, "my whole life I've done what I'm supposed to do, now I'd like to maybe do something for myself…just cuz I'm middle-aged don't mean I wanna sit around my house and watch TV…. I wanna live the real life…I wanna live my life close to the bone." That was how I'd felt for years. And how I felt most especially right at this moment during this next kiss.

Mackenzie kissed me thoroughly and sweetly and with such conveyed tenderness. I kissed her back like a hungry orphan approaches nursing. Never had I enjoyed kissing or being kissed…not like this. When our kiss reached a shared stopping point, Mackenzie paused eye to eye and studied me. I licked my lips for fear I would waste something left there.

"That was the most wonderful thing that has happened to me in a long long time," she proclaimed. "You o.k. with this?" she asked.

"I'm more than o.k. But thanks," I replied with as much tenderness as I could express in my voice as well as my facial expressions. She was kind to ask. "Is Jack Daniels acceptable?" My reference was to the drink she wanted.

"Yes, please," she replied as she clasped both hands over her heart in supplication.

I thought a shot of Jack Daniels was in order, as well. She followed me into the kitchen, not far behind. And she was quick to both notice and to grab my outstretched left hand. I held her nearby as I got out two shot glasses and the bottle of Jack. We lifted our glasses and toasted without a word. We both knew what we were toasting. And then we had another. Another toast. And another long slow lazy kiss. The type of kiss that knows no time or limits. Afterwards she put both of her strong arms around me and held me close while she kissed me on my left cheek. I didn't ever want to move. She must have sensed that, because she held me and held me and neither of us uttered what could be considered a word.

FOURTEEN: Fences

It was only five o'clock in the morning. The sun had not even considered emerging yet, but I was wide awake. The previous evening had ended all too soon with Mackenzie's departure. Saying goodbye was something neither of us seemed to want. She seemed aware of the leap I was making. I guess she thought I needed time to digest what was happening. Or maybe she needed that. I'd eaten dinner in silence and had read a few chapters of a novel. Then I'd drifted off to sleep re-enacting those tender kisses in my mind. I awoke with thoughts of Mackenzie mulling around inside my head. Everything about her was now pulling me in like a gravity field. The way the water had dripped from her bare breast demanded that my eyes open. Her tanned skin that I'd noticed through the holes in her Levi's was calling me to hurdle fences. I had no map for this uncharted territory, yet I felt like Magellan on a quest for gold. Here I was in the dark of my new home planning my next move in yet another life. Another life altogether.

Somehow, I'd managed to share several passionate kisses with a member of the same sex without freaking out. How could I freak out? Kissing her felt so right. My whole body remembered every minute detail of it all. I replayed it over and over in my memory until sunlight started to filter into my bedroom. I wanted to roll over and find her under the thick layers of covers in my four-poster bed. Maybe, just maybe that could be arranged. I had to try.

"Sorry to call you so early," I started, as she answered the phone with a groggy sleep-induced voice with which I was unfamiliar.

"That's o.k. Dear," she replied, and I was glad that I'd not needed to identify myself and glad that she'd called me my new and endearing nickname. "What's going on? We still riding this mornin'?" she yawned with hope punctuating her words.

"Maybe," I answered sounding mysterious without meaning to do so.

"You all right?" she asked with the hope I'd heard in her voice shifting to worry.

"No, I most certainly am NOT all right!" I declared. The air hung stiff. I could feel her mind fluttering to understand. Mine was busy searching my vocabulary for the words to ask her what I wanted desperately to ask. Most of the time I used the telephone I knew instinctively exactly what to say and how to say it to elicit the desired response. This time I had just dialed Mackenzie's number by heart and was winging it. I could feel both of our eyes and our thoughts darting.

"Did I do something wrong?" She placated.

"Yes, you did. First of all, you stopped kissing me. Secondly, you went home." I stated with the relief that came from being direct. Now I worried that she might not feel the same about it all.

I could feel her blue eyes take focus even though I couldn't see them over the phone. I heard the smile return to her voice as she said playfully, "Your Honor, I would like to state for the record that YOU stopped kissing me. And I felt that I should go home. I didn't want to misstep."

"Yeah, but I wanted you to stay..." I ended my sentence hanging.

She moaned and I realized that I had indeed awakened her. "I'm right here," she said.

"But that's part of the problem," I proceeded carefully. "You see, I want you right here in this big ole warm bed with me under all these covers." I had vaulted ahead and made my advances crystal clear.

"You sure about that?" She asked. "Cause that could be easily arranged."

"Do I impress you as the wishy-washy type?" I asked, knowing the answer to my own question. I had nurtured that strong self-assured woman image for years and I knew precisely how to get my point across to people when it mattered. It mattered now.

63

"You impress me. But not as wishy-washy," she replied. "You impress me as a woman who…"

I purposely interrupted her with, "Mackenzie, please come over here…right now…and get in this bed and kiss me some more."

"You won't have to ask twice," was all she said before the dial tone told me she was on her way. I wondered if I had time to brew coffee. My teeth had to be brushed first. I was a flurry of activity and the sun was barely visible over the Georgia horizon.

Her truck barreled down my driveway as if en route to a fire. In a sense, she was. I unlocked the door, left it slightly ajar, and slipped out of my terrycloth robe and back under the covers. They were still warm.

She found the open door and let herself in as I had intended.

"Lock the door behind you," I commanded. "And hurry. You know where I am," I said as I stretched to reach the cinnamon candle on my headboard. It was a big one with three wicks, and when she came in the room I was still stretched and twisted away from her lighting the last wick. She handed me the magnolia she'd picked en route. I thanked her, smelled the blossom, deposited it beside the candle, and stood naked to greet her.

She trembled and looked directly into my eyes.

"Do you have any idea how much I have wanted this?" She inquired.

"Why don't you see if you can explain it all to me," I countered playfully as I began to kiss the muscles in her graceful neck. Her breathing said she liked what I was doing. She moaned as I began to unbutton her shirt. Only three of the buttons were buttoned. Good thing because I had plans that didn't include clothes. Her shirt fell helplessly to the floor. Jeans followed. She had on no underclothes…not even any socks.

"Get dressed in a hurry?" I asked knowingly.

"Yeah, you see this woman in need woke me up with a phone call," she smiled. Goosebumps paraded all over her body as I kissed her neck just under her ear. At the same time I ran my fingers through her silky black hair. It smelled fresh like rain. She wore body oil and it smelled soft yet strong just like she was. I ran my fingers through her hair on both sides of her head and kissed her eagerly and hungrily. She pulled away from my mouth, and with her hands sliding down my bare back, she began to kiss her way down my stomach and onto the outside of my leg. When she reached my ankle, she switched to the inside of my leg, and then made her way up. This was making me crazy. But she knew it was what I desperately wanted. She kissed her way down my other leg and then back up. She lingered in places. Too long. I could hardly stand the passage of time, yet I wanted to savor all the sensations that it held.

"When she stood up, I almost gasped at the sight of her. Her body was stunning. So strong, yet so feminine. Like a work of art, she stood before me. I had imagined how she would look naked. I had seen her breasts that day in the water. She looked better than I ever could have anticipated. Now I was beginning to understand all that men must find appealing about a woman's body. She was magnificent. And she wanted me more with each touch, each kiss, and each breath that escaped our mouths when they were not touching. I pulled her mouth to mine and her hair brushed across my nipple as it traveled. Wanting her was starting to hurt. I'd never felt this kind of unending foreplay and I longed for it to culminate.

"You are wonderful and beautiful..." I declared.

"And starving," she said as she traced my breast with one hand and led me gently with her onto the bed and under the bedfull of covers.

"Me too," I smiled, "I woke up that way."

"You are not the only one, dear," she said as I pulled her on top of me. She shuddered.

"I like it when you call me that," I whispered as her mouth closed around mine in a kiss. I felt as if a protective cocoon was being spun over all of me. Especially my heart.

"You are dear to me...you do know that don't you?"
She asked with eyes locked on mine as a tear escaped me.

"I'm starting to realize that," I said as she straddled me. I
thought I would explode.

"Good," she replied as she pulled back and looked in my eyes
for what seemed like forever. She kissed my neck...sucking
both sides tenderly before returning to my mouth. I hungrily
kissed back and arched myself into her.

"Please, touch me," I found myself pleading in every way I
could and pulling her hands towards me. I slammed my head
backwards into the pillows and pushed my hips towards her.
What she did next can best be explained as tender internal
fireworks. Explosions of pleasure inside me. They
overlapped. If it had felt any better...any of it...my heart
would have exploded right then and there. The pleasure was
almost unbearable. She was masterful...like a skilled musician
caressing a well-tuned and valuable violin. She knew precisely
how to touch me. I screamed out into the morning over and
over again. Sweat trickled between us unsure to whom it
belonged. The smile that had been in her voice was now in her
kiss.

"Come here, Honey," I begged as I pulled her face to mine. I'd
never called anyone "Honey" before and wanted her to have
her own special name. Because she was in a class ALL BY
HERSELF.

We rested with her head on my chest. My heart was beating
like a happy little drum after two hours of ecstasy that had
seemed like minutes. Minutes that were frozen in my mind
forever. I caught my breath, held her tight as if she might try to
escape. She didn't.

"Water," I explained my need with one word. Now I had
gotten my second wind and she was in trouble.

"Can I have some?" She asked as she brushed the tears
wrought in pleasure from my flushed face.

I gulped my share and handed the glass to her. While she sat
up to drink, I wrapped myself around her and began to kiss

everything I could. She smelled like me except for the rain oil. She stretched out to return the glass to the bedside. The candle flickered. She reached out to me wantingly. I did what I thought might satisfy her. She arched her hips toward me wanting more and more. I gave everything I could imagine. Finally she stopped asking for more. As her body shook with relief she pulled me up to look into her eyes. Eye to eye she registered pleasure with me watching. Tears welled up warm and salty in her eyes. When I kissed her this time it was all different.

"What's the matter?" I worried out loud.

"Nothing, Sandy." A long contented sigh punctuated her words. "Everything about this is perfect…every little detail of it." "You still all right?" she wondered about me and the fence I'd just climbed.

"I will most certainly never be the same again…. and I'm not remotely looking back," I declared. She seemed reassured by what the words I'd used to explain myself. I tried my best to calm her fears as I caressed her face and kissed the trail of her tears. I had never before tasted a woman's tears. I had never tasted many of the things I tasted that morning in my bed. But no misgivings ever entered my mind. This could not possibly ever stop if I had anything to do with it all. Once I knew she was asleep, I walked naked to the kitchen and poured us both cups of coffee. I put cream in hers and enjoyed knowing how she likes her coffee as well as knowing how she likes everything else. Everything else. She slept for only about five minutes. I watched the air fill her lungs until her blue eyes opened. I filled my mouth with her coffee and kissed it into hers. She giggled, but she let me give her the whole cup that way. All the smells and all the sensations and all the knowing and kind looks made me feel so full and so desirable and so much at peace and at home.

The clock frightened me. "Eleven forty-five! Am I making you late for shoeing?

"Nope," was all she seemed to have the energy to say.

I was puzzled that she didn't have any appointments.

"Had to cancel my work this morning…one of my best customers had an emergency," she smiled. "A fire."

"Wanna ride then?" I asked with all the enthusiasm of the schoolgirl I now felt like.

"No…I want to hold you. And I want to sleep," she said. "And when we wake up I want to make love to you over and over again and fall asleep in your arms."

"You bet…. what a fabulous idea…but I need to feed my horses first," I remembered. "Brunch."

"Sorry," she offered. "Blame it on the farrier."

"Nope, this was my idea," I admitted as I pulled the covers up over her face-down spread-eagle body as sleep seeped over her like a wave on the sand.

I hurried into my bathrobe and sandals and out to the horses. I fed them as fast as I could, said "Hello" and returned to my bed and my lover. My bed smelled like sex and it smelled like her. What a great place to rest. She rolled over and wrapped her arms around me and pulled me close. My back was to her and her soft breath on my neck rhythmically rocked me to sleep. As I began to drift off, I reflected on how good this encounter had felt…how good it still felt. And I remembered ones with others. With men who had left me feeling used and alone. Good sex, but sex that left out this part. This close part I felt now. We fit together. I couldn't wait to wake up now that she was in my bed.

She belonged right where she was. In my bed. I belonged there in her arms. I thought she was already sleeping, but she kissed my back and said words that stopped my heart, "Sweet dreams, Sandy." The only other person who had ever said that to me was my mother when I was a child drifting off to sleep. I could get so used to this. This was another life. Another life that I had brought upon myself. One that I wholeheartedly embraced.

"Sweet dreams to you," I replied with a sigh. The nap was divine…the kind of sleep that only follows meaningful intimacy. And when I awoke my body was registering pleasure...slow steady love making that had picked up where we had left off earlier. She wasn't forceful about it. She touched me and waited for my body to respond. I was reacting physically long before I was fully awake and it was so erotic. Being touched... being loved into awareness. Over and over my body loved what she did to me. Every now and then she would look to me for a reaction. My every fiber told her that what she did, what she was doing, and what she would yet do was exquisite. It was like the taste of a rich full-bodied fruit-flavored oak–aged fine red wine. And it lingered just like an elegant wine in my mouth and in my soul and in my heart.

We made love to each other for hours. Time was of no consequence except that it afforded us expression of what we felt for each other. Like a well-written symphony, my passion for Mackenzie crescendoed. I had never spent an entire day in bed before. Except when I was sick with the flu or something. And I was feeling ever so well. We had gotten up, never for long and never at the same time. To blow out the candles. To go to the bathroom. To open a bottle of wine. To snack. But all day long and well into the night, we loved each other in every way our bodies and our minds could imagine. It was incomparably wonderful...it was hedonism at its finest and I didn't feel the least bit guilty about wallowing in all that pleasure.

Next morning when I awoke, there she was in my arms in my bed and firmly rooted in my life and my heart. Like a repotted plant she now had all kinds of room to grow. And she possessed all the nourishment I could ever attempt to supply. All my life I had longed for this. Just exactly this.

"Morning, my dear," she whispered as she peppered my neck softly with her mouth. Her hands tracing my shoulders and my legs. "Are we spending another day in bed?" she asked with a moan remembering.

"We better not," I said. "People will talk."

"Bet they already are," she said, "Since my truck has not moved overnight and all this candlelight flooding the curtains."

"Let's give em more to talk about then," I said as I straddled her and began the ritual of intimacy all over again. We started that day out right. My body felt tingly all over for hours after she had driven away. Too bad she had shoeing to do. I could have easily kept her captive in my bed for another day.

"Be careful today," was my admonition on her answering machine. "You have become very precious to me, Mackenzie." I smiled as I held the phone to my chest listening to the dial tone. My heart was full and my body was purring inside and out.

FIFTEEN: Contentment and Flowers

I decided to go horseback riding. I wanted to go on a long ride all by myself. This time I would ride Zippy. She was my favorite horse to ride, after all. And most of the time when Mackenzie and I rode, I had to forfeit my favorite steed. I felt full and Zippy was tall and athletic and intuitive. She had to be able to sense how I felt. She trotted as if floating. She was barely touching the ground. My spirits floated as well…barely touching reality as they traveled. After feeling so intimate so closely connected to another human being, you can really bask in the solitary moments that inevitably are going to follow. I wanted to revisit the place where Mackenzie and I had splashed and played in the water of the river. My heart wanted to spend all day revisiting and remembering.

But when we reached the river, all I wanted to do was to sit and think. Water seems to have that effect on me. As I held the reins in my hand and watched my horse eat grass in spite of the bit, I reflected back on it all. Like well-worn home movies, my mind projected so many memories that had been recorded during the last few days of my life. A gentle breeze blew through my hair and fingered Zippy's mane as it rippled the surface of the water. What a perfect day! In every respect, this day was perfect. What a lovely turn my life had taken. I usually saw things coming. This bend in the road had taken me totally by surprise, but I was reveling in the surprise and in the events that seemed to have overtaken me.

On the way home, we cantered for miles. Cantering in synch with a strong horse can be compared to the closeness of lovemaking. Not that it is anything sexual. But it is two beings working as one. We traveled for miles without a sound except for an occasional snort from Zippy along with my breathing and the squishing sound of her hooves digging into the ground underneath us. Miles without words and thoughts that covered miles. I was finally finding my niche. And I'd never realized that I had not previously possessed a niche of my own. At forty-two years of age I felt like a teenager. I felt as if I'd found myself. This woman who was on a horse enjoying an easy gallop…this woman enjoying her body and

71

'her body' earlier…this was the real me. Flying through the air on the back of my favorite horse, I vowed to keep following myself wherever this path led.

When I returned home, my heart stopped. Blood was pouring from Princess Jazmine's right eye. Her eyelid was hanging on by only a thread of skin and she was pacing nervously around the paddock. In the excitement of her stable mate's departure earlier, she must have hit her head or cut her eye on something. I tied Zippy to the hitching rail and ran in the house to call the vet.

Clayton answered on the third ring. "I'll be right there. Five minutes," he promised with a tone in his voice that was reassuring. "Try and keep her calm, and do not let her rub on anything," he added before he hung up the phone.

I ran back and unsaddled Zippy. I led her by the reins. Into the corral she went without being brushed down. That was a first for me. But I wanted to halter her sister before the vet arrived. P. J. wasn't overly willing to be caught. Shortly after I snapped the halter into place and gathered up the slack of the cotton lead line, Clayton's truck came into view. What a welcome sight a veterinarian can be when you are standing there waiting with your injured horse.

"What is it with you two and hurting your eyes?" He said to the horse as he took stock of her injury. "This is gonna be fun." Only a vet would think this sort of thing could be fun. "I'm going to sew this up with her standing," he informed me "But I'm going to have to heavily sedate her so you can hold her still." As he was talking, he gave one shot in a vein in one side of her neck followed by another in the other side. I always marveled at the way a vet could find a vein and administer the shot so handily. Princess Jazmine hardly flinched at either shot.

"Good girl," I said as I praised my horse.

"You just wanted to see me again, right?" Clayton said…this time addressing me instead of the horse.

"Not hardly," I sighed bluntly. My response really did explain how I felt on many levels, but I didn't mean it to sound so cold.

"Wow, you really do know how to wound a fella's ego." He admitted as he listened to the horse's heartbeat through his stethoscope.

"That's not what I meant," I said, which was only half true. "I meant that the horse needed you here…not me." I was digging an even deeper hole for myself.

"So you did want to see me again," he said, putting unwanted words in my mouth. I hate it when people do that.

"Well…" I said ambiguously on purpose. I was never good at pretenses. Especially not with all I had recently begun to feel for Mackenzie. Clayton Thompson was the furthest thing from my mind right now. And he didn't even have a clue. That 'fresh meat' feeling was back. And it rubbed me the wrong way that he was mixing business with pleasure. It was unprofessional and it made me feel extremely uncomfortable. "Calm down, now." I said as I gave a slow steady pull on the lead rope.

"Talkin' to me or to the horse?" He'd donned a headlamp to help him see how to sew, but now I was in the spotlight.

"Both!" I blurted out sincerely. My eyes punctuated my one word admonition. He was hard to train, like most men. But he did catch on after that. He silently and skillfully sewed her eyelid back into place. He then detailed her follow up care and tallied up my bill for the treatment without looking at me once.

He watched from the front seat of his truck while I walked back from the house with my checkbook. He watched me write out the check and hand it to him.

"Thank you, Clayton…and thanks for getting here so fast, again."

"You are very welcome," he replied. "Will you go out with me again?" He asked and then he looked up at me like a scared puppy that needed love.

"Clayton," I said with startling firmness in my tone, "I have to tell you that this makes me very uncomfortable."

"What?" he asked with a shell-shocked look on his face. The man was handsome and maybe he'd never been turned down.

"This mixing business with pleasure. It makes me uncomfortable." I explained only half of the picture to him. "You are a skilled vet, and I'm indebted to you for what you did for this horse. But I paid you for that, and my going out on a date with you is not going to be a tip. I'm not a commodity to be traded!" I could feel my face redden as the apparent anger in my words registered on his face.

"You are right. I didn't mean it that way." He melted in the way that only innocence could enable him to do. "I just keep blowin' it with you, don't I...it's just that..."

"Plus, I find myself falling in love with someone else these last few days," I interrupted and blurted out what I wanted to shout from the mountaintops.

"Really," He said as he took off his hat and ducked all the way into the truck. "Hats off to the lucky fella." He was smiling, but I knew he was not remotely happy. And he still had no clue about anything. He just drove away. None too soon, as far as I was concerned.

As soon as he left, I went in the back yard and picked a handful of wildflowers and tied them up with a hay string. Then I penned a note to Mackenzie, relieved to talk to her, though it was only in a note.

"Thank you for taking my hand. Thank you for leading me into such a wonderful place: your life. I do not want to scare you away. But I do want to know you more and more. I want to ride with you still. I want to sit and talk with you. And I want to fix dinner for you tonight...if you do not have other plans. Come as you are and we will shower together. I still want you." I signed the note and then I read over what I'd written. It only began to tell her all I felt. I took the flowers and the note and put them in a coffee can by her door. I hoped they would not wilt too much before she came home. This was fun. And this was different, too. I'd never given flowers to a lover before. I liked it. I hoped she would like the surprise.

It was almost six-thirty when she appeared at my door. I imagined that she'd fed her horses and Mitch before she left home. Her smile ran down the driveway ahead of her. She was positively beaming!

"You ARE wonderful!" She exclaimed. "Nobody has ever given me flowers before." She said, much to my amazement.

"Well then, things are changing for you, too." I teased as she grabbed me, pulled me close, and thanked me in person with a long slow thorough kiss. She was covered with dirt but underneath it all her face still smelled like me. I wanted to seep into her skin just like the telltale smell of the horses that she'd been touching all day. She had a dirt beard made out of red Georgia clay. She was really dirty, but she was no less beautiful underneath it all.

"Good day at the office?" I asked with a smile that demanded its rightful presence on my face.

"Yeah…nice horses," she smiled back. "Good thing, too cause my mind was totally somewhere else. It was right here with you all day long." She punctuated her words with another lingering kiss. "And don't you worry about scaring me away. That ain't gonna happen."

"Good." I ended that thought and told her all about Princess Jazmine and her eye injury. She wanted to see the horse. I liked the fuss she made over me and over my horses. You could tell it was sincere. P.J. hates for anyone to hold her head in their hands, yet she let Mackenzie do just that. I can't blame her. The woman has a commanding way of holding you. A way that makes you not want to budge. Her hands are so powerful yet so gentle. I liked watching her with my horse.

We finished up with the horses and made our way into the cabin. My home. And it had begun to feel like home in many ways lately.

"Sandy, are you o.k. with all this?" She asked as I cut off her words with a kiss. "You know, being intimate with a woman for the first time and all...that was the first time, wasn't it?"

"You couldn't tell?" I asked. Any time you sleep with someone you're unsure of yourself. Especially if you care. I cared. "And yes, that was the first time."

"No, I couldn't tell. You're a quick study," she said with a naughty grin and a raised eyebrow. "That was divine."

"Listen, I know what I did. And I have no regrets. I even told Clayton," I declared with pride. "Well not in so many words, but I turned him down for a date and told him I was..." choosing my words carefully "beginning to care for someone else."

She looked pleased but teased me, "You didn't tell me about that. Anyone I know?"

"Yeah, like you couldn't tell that either!" I chuffed. "Thirsty?"

"Yes, I'm. Work does that...and what I would really love is an ice cold beer!" She revealed.

"Miller Light or Budweiser?" I asked as I checked the fridge. She reached for the Budweiser and handed me a plastic bag she'd brought in. It contained two t-bone steaks she'd brought for us to cook on the grill. I could tell she relished my company as much as I did hers.

We sat on the porch and drank beer. I told her about the vet's advances and his wounded retreat. I also told her I couldn't think about anything else but her all day long. I asked her how she managed to get that old without anyone ever giving her flowers.

"Hey, I'm not that old. Just cause I'm two years older than you does not mean..."

I interrupted with, "Yeah, but forty-four, and no flowers. That's unthinkable."

Then she proceeded to tell me a little bit about her past relationships. People who used her. People who played games…all women except for her high school boyfriend. All had been too self-absorbed to give her much of anything…including flowers. She said that she admired me because I'm straightforward about things and because I thought about her and how to give not take. This woman was really something else. When she propped up her feet, I instinctively pulled off her work boots. My dad used to like that after a long workday. Her eyes softened.

"See what I mean," she said as she affectionately touched my arm.

We drank and we talked and I pulled her into the bathroom and peeled off her dirty clothes. She wore so much dirt on her arms that it still looked like she had on a shirt when she was naked. We laughed at that thought, and I pulled her into the shower with me. I turned on the water, which made her laugh out loud since I was fully clothed.

"I want you to undress me in the water," I flirted. She wholeheartedly agreed and began to do so without hesitation.

"I wanted to undress you that day in the river," I confessed.

"Then I think you have homosexual tendencies." She diagnosed.

"Nurture them…would you please?" I begged. She kissed me long and deeply. A type of kiss that only lovers share. Good lovers. We stood under the warm cascade and kissed hungrily. I took a thick jade washcloth and carefully covered all of her body with soap and warm water. Her muscles glistened clean after the soapy water did its job. She stood there with her eyes closed as I washed her…then spread out and pressed her palms onto the shower wall while I caressed and scrubbed her back. Her strong arms and her back and her legs…everywhere I touched was beautiful. She preened. Washing her and planning to make love to her was making my mouth water. My touching her was arousing us both, so we abandoned the hard porcelain for my unmade bed. We barely dried each other off.

Hours once again passed like seconds. We ended up grilling our steaks in the dark with a flashlight. I held her tight from behind and couldn't seem to stop kissing her while she cooked. She didn't seem to mind. Her appetite seemed insatiable. Previous lovers, especially my whining ex-husband, had always left me wanting more. Sex had been a chore to them and a frequent source of contention. It felt so good for somebody to want me that way again. In many ways this felt like the first time anyone had ever really hungered for me. This woman couldn't seem to get enough of me. She wore me out.

"I love being with you like this," I declared bravely, as the last ounce of strength seemed to drip out of my weary body.

After a long pause, she said deliberately, "Sandy," she looked in my eyes in the candlelight and after she had my eyes fixed on hers she finished, "I love you, too."

"I guess I can't scare you away, after all." I mumbled.

"Not a chance." She said as she both kissed me and held me close all over. I could hardly tolerate this much comfort in one place. As I drifted off to sleep I realized that we both wanted all of the same things in life: home and horses and comfort and sweet dreams.

Morning came too soon. The alarm I'd set for her rudely interrupted our sleeping. Just as I remembered my deep-seated hatred for alarm clocks, I realized that Mackenzie was still in my bed. Again. Both of her arms were still wrapped around me and she kissed me in the middle of my back. She began to caress me and we picked up right where we had left off before we had fallen asleep. After an hour or so, we decided to force ourselves out of the bed and make coffee. We dressed each other…kissing and touching all along the way. I dressed her in the clean clothes she'd brought along and threw her dirty ones in my washer.

We sat on the porch and watched the horses. Our coffee was good. And we sat as close as we could to each other. The sense of touch had suddenly become so important to us. It was a way to share what we both felt. I threw hay to the horses and

I could feel her eyes on me the whole time. When I returned to the porch, she pulled me onto her lap and squeezed me tightly. We sat there just like that and drank more coffee. I felt at home. After what seemed like too short a morning, she hopped in her truck with a smile.

"Gotta go. Horses are calling." She winked. "Can I call you tonight?"

"You better!" I admonished and kissed her goodbye through the open truck window. She kissed back aggressively yet lingered tenderly at the end.

As she drove away I couldn't stop watching long after she was gone. Tears clouded my vision. My heart felt young again. And full.

Now what would I do today? It had to be something good. Something that would occupy my busy mind. I'd so much to think about. And all of it was good. This cabin had felt so much love over the years. But I was just beginning to feel. As if for the first time, I was in love. Deeply, helplessly, and fearlessly in love.

SIXTEEN: Horse Farm

If this was going to be a respectable horse breeding business, I needed to buy one more horse. A breeding stallion. Just the thing to occupy my busy brain. I had an Arabian stallion in mind, and he was even for sale. At least he had been when I began planning this venture several months ago. I popped his promotional video in the VCR and watched him prance around again. Then I phoned his owner. He was still for sale even though there had been several people who had shown a strong interest in him. A twelve-year old stallion without much of a show record was harder to promote. But I liked the fact that he had not been shown much. Most people do not realize what all goes on behind the scenes at horse shows. Bathing, shaving, oiling, sanding hooves, and cruel training methods are commonplace. It takes a toll on the emotional health of any horse…especially a stallion. And if he has been used for breeding a great deal, his hind legs have usually been strained.

The owner and I agreed on a price and she faxed me a contract. Thanks to my stock options, profit sharing, early retirement, savings, and the sale of my house in Ohio, I did have a little money to spend. As I looked over the horse's papers, I wondered what Mackenzie would think of him. I didn't know much about feet. Maybe she would be able to evaluate him based on the video. Plus, I had several contingencies written into the contract since I'd not yet seen the horse in person. He was a well-bred horse and he was stunning. My girls would hopefully love him and become the foundations for my breeding program. I'd bought several books on horse breeding. But my mind had been too busy to read. I remembered my neighbor the nurse. She knew a thing or two about breeding horses.

Just as I thought her name, someone knocked on my door. It was Becca.

"Hey, Becca…I was just thinking about you."

"Time for a visit, I thought." She said with a smile. This time she handed me a small pewter picture frame. It was such a perfect gift and I thought instantly about Mackenzie.

"You know you can come over any time. And you don't have to bring a present." I reminded her. "Want some sweet tea?" I asked.

"That'll be great," she agreed "and you can tell me all about your new girlfriend."

I gulped.

"It's fine by me," she said as she took my arm, "not that you need my permission." She added. "I don't mean to be the nosey neighbor, but you do live right next door and her truck was here all night a couple of times."

"No, it's all right, Becca." I smiled as I poured our tea. "I have been ready to explode because I haven't been able to share all this with anyone, yet." I was relieved to hear that she wasn't going to disapprove of my liaison with Mackenzie. Not that it mattered to me what anyone thought. But I'd grown fond of Becca, and now I had a confidante with which to share my happy news.

The dam burst. "She is really amazing, Becca." Where would I begin? "She is fun and romantic, and her body...you should see how muscular she is underneath..." I stopped mid-sentence because Becca's face had reddened. "Sorry, Becca, I didn't mean to embarrass you."

"Hey, it really is o.k.," she sighed with a reassuring look on her face. "I'm the one sticking my nose in your business," she said. "I was a little surprised though, since I thought you were straight."

"I was...or at least I thought I was all along." I confessed. "But I have been so powerfully drawn to this woman," I said, pausing to search for the words. "It doesn't matter to me whether she is a man or a woman...it only matters that I express what I feel in every way I can find to express it." I hoped that made sense. The look on my face and the feeling in my words must have sufficed.

"Well good for you!" She exclaimed. "Life is too short to not be happy...and I told you that you'd like her."

Becca had, after all, referred me to Mackenzie. She'd been an unknowing matchmaker when she sent me to secure a farrier.

"Becca, being with Mackenzie is the most wonderful thing," I said with a girlish grin. "For the first time in my life, it feels like nothing is missing in this relationship."

"I can see that on your face." She did seem happy for me. "Does Mac feel the same way?" she asked, calling her by the nickname I'd chosen not to use.

"Yeah, I think so…" I said dreamily.

"Sandy, I'm well aware of Mac's good qualities…and not just as a farrier." Becca reminded me. "You WILL encounter your share of resistance here, though…. this is the Bible belt, you know."

"We'll deal with it." I stated succinctly. "But I'm glad to know you approve."

"Thought you could put her picture in that frame." She said as she pointed to the pewter picture frame she'd brought.

We took our sweet tea out onto the porch and I told her all about the wonders of my new lover. I left out many of the details that were way too personal to share with anyone. Good sex with someone always has those secret ingredients. But this was so much more than just good sex. Even though we had only known each other for a short time, Mackenzie and I'd formed a strong bond. Becca understood it all and applauded me for being courageous enough to break with convention.

"You really are starting a new life here…in more ways than one." She observed. "This isn't overwhelming you, is it?" She asked with concern permeating her words.

"No, not so far," I replied, "and I really don't think it will." I explained. "Who better to understand how to please a woman than another woman?" I added. Someone had told me that once. Now I understood the significance of the statement. Intimately.

"Good for you!" She exclaimed again, as she set down her empty glass. "Thanks for the sweet tea…but I wanna get home before Tim does." She said as she rose to leave. "And thanks for sharing your news…. I really am happy for you two."

"You are quite welcome." I beamed. "I could hardly wait to tell…and you're the perfect one."

"Tell that farrier I said to treat you right," she said with a smile. "Good people like you don't come along every day."

"Thanks, Becca. See ya later." She had called me 'good people.' That made me feel even happier.

"All that time living in Ohio, and you still know how to make good sweet tea." She said with a contagious giggle in her voice.

Making sweet tea is an art. You have to add the sugar and lemon while the tea is still hot. If not, you may as well just pour the whole pitcher of it right down the drain. It isn't worth drinking unless you do it that way. Only a person of southern heritage can understand that. So I knew what Becca had meant in her compliment. Plus she'd said that I was a "good person." Coming from her, the words meant a great deal to me. I'd come to admire my new neighbor deeply, especially now that I'd confided my newfound sexuality with her. Now someone else in the world knew how strong my feelings for Mackenzie had become. I only hoped she would continue to respond in kind because now I couldn't begin to imagine my life without Mackenzie playing a key role in it.

The phone rang a little after six-o'clock and it was my mother. When she asked why I answered the phone on the first ring, I told her. Only I left out the part about Mackenzie being a woman. She cautioned me not to get involved with anyone too fast. "Yeah, yeah." I said allowing my annoyance to be heard. No matter how old I became, my mother would always treat me like a child. I could just picture myself in my sixties hearing my ninety-year-old Mama caution me about life as if I'd just begun to live it. Some mothers just never relinquish that throne. Mine was obviously an unyielding despot. When the phone rang again, I thought it was Mama with an afterthought.

"Hey there, good-looking! Whatcha got cooking?" It was the voice I'd ached to hear all day. It wasn't my mother. I loved the sound of the smile in Mackenzie's voice.

"Nothing, so far." I admitted. "I've been busy talking with Becca about someone special in my life."

"Me?" She asked, with uncharacteristic insecurity.

"Oh, yeah…and she approves." I declared boldly.

"So Sandy," she said changing gears, "Could I interest you in going out to dinner with me?"

"You could…but only if you will do two things. Pick me up at seven and take me home with you after dinner."

"I accept." She said emphatically and hung up the phone before I could say another word. I fed the horses and medicated Princess Jazmine's eye as told. Then I discarded my clothes in haste before jumping into the shower. Same place where Mackenzie had stretched out for scrubbing. But this shower was rushed. So was packing my duffel bag. I did throw in a scented pine candle in a glass jar with a lid. Even though this wasn't Christmas, it was a special occasion. I had just invited myself over to spend the night with my 'girlfriend' for the first time. And she had wholeheartedly accepted. I had never had a girlfriend before. I do not recall ever being this happy either.

I had just finished getting ready and uncorking the wine when her truck appeared in my driveway. The first sip was for me. I wondered if she would want beer or wine. I could tell by the look on her face that she wanted me. Her eyes were fixed on me through the open window all the way down the driveway. That focus made my heart race. My pulse quickened along with her steps as she bounded from her truck and before I knew it, she was standing in my doorway. Without a word, we kissed. I inadvertently gave her some of my wine in the process. The kiss was long and knowing. I could tell she'd missed me. The night before us held promise.

"MMM, that was good!" She proclaimed.

"What, the kiss or the wine?" I asked teasingly.

"Both." She said with confidence. "May I have another?"

"Another wha…" I began to ask, but she interrupted me with her mouth. She cupped her arm around my waist and under my shirt. She had touched bare skin and it gave me goose bumps.

"You hungry?" She wondered out loud.

"Yeah, I am," was my honest reply, "and I want some food, too." I elaborated as I poured her a glass of wine. Flirting with a new lover is so much fun, and I was in my element now.

We flirted shamelessly with each other and shared a couple of glasses of wine before we closed up my house and left for dinner. In the process, she told me all about her day of shoeing horses. I told her about my stallion shopping and about my girl talk with Becca. Her face turned red when I relayed the part about her body. She had somehow failed to notice just how good her own body looked. And she had called me 'good looking' earlier on the phone.

She opened the truck door for me and kissed me as I fumbled for the seat belt. While kissing me she reached into the back and pulled out a bouquet of flowers wrapped in green paper. My name was on the little card and the tulips smelled sweet. What a welcome surprise! When she slid into the driver's seat, she handed me a card that had been on the dashboard. She didn't seem to forget any of love's trappings, and I hoped I wasn't dreaming. No one had treated me this way in a very long time. I was wallowing in all the attention. Mackenzie pulled me close and looked me in the eye as she said, "I just want to remind you how very much you have come to mean to me, Sandy."

My response seemed only natural. I kissed her and our souls touched. Not for the first time. This woman had become a part of me. I doubted I would ever be the same again. Did not want to be the same again.

When we arrived at the little Italian restaurant, the
maitre de ushered us to our table. More yellow tulips. And
another card with my name on it. But this time there was a
little package wrapped in silver wrapping paper perched in my
salad bowl. Tears welled up in my eyes and spilled down onto
my lap as I realized she had been to the restaurant already to
set this all in motion.

"Open it," she said softly, "It's for you." As she spoke, she
scooted her chair closer to mine. The waiter lit our hurricane
candle and disappeared on cue.

I was speechless. Her forethought was making my heart melt
into a little heap before me. The package contained a silver
pendant and the printed tag read, "Kuan Yin, Chinese Goddess
of Compassion, Kindness, and Love, her name translates as
She-Who-Harkens-to-the-Cries-of-the-World." I took each end
of the silk cord and tied it around my neck. She dabbed my
tears with her cloth napkin and we ordered our food soon after.
Time seemed to proceed in slow motion. I felt right where I
belonged. She held my hand across the table. If anyone
noticed or whispered objections, neither of us heard nor cared.
When we stood to leave, the waiter handed her the tulips.
Mackenzie said under her breath so only I could hear, "Good,
'cause I have plans for these."

My knees grew weak. Once we were alone outside, she kissed
me as a way of revealing at least a part of her plans for the rest
of our evening. "Are you always like this?" I wondered out
loud.

"Like what?" She inquired with a worried tone to her voice.

"This romantic?" I clarified.

"I'm hopeless," She confessed. "I hope you don't mind."

"Do I look retarded?" I asked her with a look on my face that
must have made her laugh.

"No," she stated emphatically, "You look lovely…it's just that
I don't want to come on too strong."

"How could anyone object to being treated this way?" I asked rhetorically.

"And how could anyone not want to make love to you?" She reminded me about my ex-husband's accusations. That was rapidly becoming a distant painful memory.

When we opened the door to her house there were more tulips. Different colors in every room, and a dozen or more of the fragrant petals were strewn on the turned-down bed covers. I could take a hint. After I told her so with a seductive kiss, it didn't take us long to find our way there. She made me lie very still face down while she caressed me all over with each petal of every tulip on the bed. Then she gently rolled me over onto my back and brought all of the rest of the flowers we had collected throughout our date into the bed. She carefully and without hurrying plucked all the petals from all the tulips and caressed my naked and quivering body with each one. And as she caressed, she kissed. It was like nothing I had ever known…to be touched that way with all those flowers. Her touch communicated so much to me about who she was and how she'd come to care for me.

We drank from the wine that had been chilling in a bucket on the nightstand. The light from the candle I had brought along flickered well into the morning. Sleep had overpowered us, at some point. Ensconced in all the comforts of her and her aura and her bed and her home, I slept. I felt her warm breath on me as she blew out the candle. She gently pulled me as close as possible to her body and to her spirit. We slept that way all night. My mother's warning totally unheeded. And unnecessary.

Morning broke early. Mackenzie was kissing me. What a sublime way to wake up! Coffee colored the air. How nice. Even though I no longer needed it to wake up, it still smelled inviting. So did Mackenzie. She woke me up by kissing me. Then she served me coffee in bed. She had a busy day of shoeing ahead. I had a horse to buy, and a fence to build. I had brought the video of the stallion for her to evaluate. But I couldn't seem to stop touching her. Or kissing her, for that matter. I had never felt this sort of hunger for another person…male or female. And I knew it would only deepen.

We watched the stallion's promotional video, and she said he looked good. He seemed sound, from what all she could see in the video. We agreed I should buy him. And she told me I needed to name my farm. For my own promotional videos someday. I hadn't even thought about a name for my place. It had always been my grandparents' cabin. Now it was mine. Plus it was en route to becoming a horse-breeding farm. One that would soon have a fence and a name and a stallion's corral.

When she took me home, I had to pry myself out of the truck. I started to walk away and she called me back. Good. Time for another kiss. Just one more. That was what she had in mind, too. But during the kiss she produced a small brown paper bag. "Don't open it until I'm gone." She warned me with a serious look on her face. But even the serious look could not eclipse the softness in her voice for me.

I waited like I'd been told until she was at the end of my driveway before I looked. Tulips. And a lock of her sleek black hair. She had gathered up some of the scented petals she'd caressed me with. And she had cut off a lock of her own hair and tied it up with a blue silk ribbon. "To remember me," was what the little note said.

The scent of tulips will always remind me of that salacious night. And the lock of her hair was a keepsake I needed. I went in my bedroom and opened the empty alabaster box I had owned for some time. In it I placed the card from my necklace, the lock of hair, and a few of the tulip petals. The rest I sprinkled under the covers of my bed. Then I sat there on the edge of the bed and cried. I just sat there speechless. I could say nothing. Not even to myself.

This was unlike anything I'd ever felt. I think I had been in love before. But not like this. The tears I cried tethered her soul to mine. And she was off…already on her way to work. She would spend her day with her clients and their horses. I would go about my day, as well. But I would live for the sound of her next breath in my ears. I thought about the tulips and the note and the lock of her hair. Like I could possibly forget any of that memorably wonderful night! Or the romantic woman that I had come to love so deeply. The one with the silky black hair. And all those tulips.

SEVENTEEN: Passing Time

The next year of my life was idyllic. It had the exact
ingredients I had sought in my recipe for cooking up a new life.
My crops flourished and so did I. The girls loved the stallion.
They picked on him at first, but now they fought over who
could graze with him. My perimeter fence was respectable. It
consisted of four by four wooden posts and six-foot high
stallion wire fence with electrical tape around the top of it all.
Each horse had its own pipe corral so that I could separate
them at feeding time. But the rest of the time they grazed
contentedly and bred whenever the mares allowed. Both of his
girls were in foal, and Onyx seemed proud of himself. I had
decided he would be better adjusted if he could be in a herd
with the girls instead of segregated. That is how it's done in
nature after all. People call it "live cover" as if humans
invented it. Plus they kept the grass eaten down.

I was becoming more and more self-sufficient. I read the
Farmer's Almanac and grew anything and everything I could.
Weather predictions always brought thoughts of my
crops…and of Mackenzie's workday. My life and previous
career in the city had become the past's distant mirage. I had
retired. But I had just begun to live. It seemed as if my
emotional life had begun long ago with that first kiss with my
dear Mackenzie.

We traded sleepovers. Each of us had a chest of drawers full of
our own clothes at the other person's house. I felt just as at
home in her house as I did in mine. Because she was there.
Sometimes, we argued over something significant enough to
keep us apart for the better part of two days. We were both
strong and stubborn women. But then one of us would grovel.
Then we would trip over who was sorrier than whom. Our
horseback rides continued most mornings…but not every day.
Sometimes we would stay in bed as long as possible. Not
sleeping. Or she would sneak outside and saddle both horses to
surprise me. We would wake up on the backs of our horses as
the sun rose on our good lives that were steadily becoming one.

Mackenzie's horseshoeing business was thriving, and I went with her and watched sometimes. It gave me such pride to watch her work. And it made me want her anew. People in town had come to realize that we were much more than good friends. Neither of us made any serious attempts to hide that fact, either. We didn't make out in public, but everyone saw our affection for each other. We refused to hide. Feeling ashamed causes human beings to hide. I was proud of her in my life. We went to a few gay bars in Atlanta. But I never felt a pull for the bar scene.

I did feel an increasing magnetic pull towards Mackenzie. And she just so happened to be a woman. I kept waiting for any of this to feel weird. I think she was afraid I would wake up one day and regret being so involved with her. I never did, and I knew I never would. Another tide that never seemed to wane was the flow of Mackenzie's romantic gestures. She was thoroughly spoiling me. I did my best to keep pace. It was fun to compete in a good way. I had always been competitive, but she had not. She did have the creative edge, though.

"Hurry up!" She said once as she led me by the hand. "I have to show you what I found up here," she urged as she pulled me up the stairs to her hayloft. I expected to see a newborn litter of kittens or chirping hatchlings. Instead it looked like something out of a magazine. No hay. Instead she'd pieced together an elaborate nest for us. She'd arranged a mattress, pillows, blankets, and a picnic fit for royalty. Wine was chilling. Soft music was playing and candles were flickering in the dusk. She pushed me down hard on the bed and pulled the evil clothing from my body. Hours passed there that will be forever etched in every recess of my heart. Those surprises were her specialty, and she was full of them. I never knew what she might spring on me next. And she loved dreaming of new ways to surprise me. I could see that on her face each time.

Clay Thompson quit asking me out a long time ago. He was civil about it, but I could tell his feelings were hurt. It must be a blow to a man's ego to see the woman he wants fall helplessly and completely in love with someone else right before his eyes. Especially when that someone else is another woman. Only Bobby Hannah had the nerve to say something about it all to my face. Even though he is a pitiful human being, I did admire him for saying it to my face. It had happened once when he'd been out to work on my tractor.

"Why you wanna take up with a woman?" He'd said. "Ain't none of us Georgia boys good enough for you?" He asked as he spat a noxious blob of tobacco juice onto the ground next to the tractor.

Never at a loss for words, I'd replied, "Georgia has nothing to do with it, Bob." I shortened his name because I'd heard he hated that. "And not that my love life has ever been any of your business, but I like making love to a woman for probably some of the same reasons you do." My words created a funny look on his face. Perplexed yet aware. "Is there anything else you need to know? From what I hear, your wife might want me to give you some pointers!"

I thought he was going to hit me. But he did the most unexpected thing. He nudged me like I was one of the boys. And he laughed out loud all the way back to his truck after I paid the bill. Men are the strangest things. I had just insulted his manhood and he was laughing. He treated me differently from then on. Other people looked at me strangely when they saw me around town. But nobody had trouble accepting my money.

People had begun to talk about my crops. Even a few of them had learned what organic farming was all about. They had taken bets on when my crops would succumb to the bugs since I didn't use conventional pesticides. Nobody ever won the money. And my cellar was full of canned tomatoes, okra, pepper relish, preserves, and everything else edible. My freezer was full of stewed corn and acre peas. I made fewer and fewer trips to the grocery store. I had even learned how to make my own soap and candles. I loved candles in my house…and in Mackenzie's.

Life had finally reached a long sought-after stability for me. Then one day in August, my peace was shattered with meteoric suddenness. Becca and Tim came to my house together around two in the afternoon on a Saturday. Becca's face tightened around the words that seemed to hurt her to utter, "Sandy, there has been an accident." Their faces told me it was bad. "Mackenzie is hurt...she is alive, but she is hurt bad." She knew I wanted the truth.

Tears instantly choked me. "What happened...how?" I fumbled over the words.

Tim went to get their car while Becca explained. Mackenzie had been shoeing a horse that had been badly abused by a previous owner. A dog had startled the horse right about the time Mackenzie bent over to pick up a tool she was using. The horse had missed the dog, but it had kicked Mackenzie squarely in the head with the shoe she'd just nailed on. Life Flight had rushed her to a hospital in Atlanta.

"Please don't let her die," I pleaded with Becca and with God. Becca's arms held me tight. "I finally found the love of my life." I gasped for air as if I too had been kicked. "Please, Becca, take me to her...take me to Mackenzie."

"We will...Tim is getting the car." She said as she tried to reassure me. "We're here to take you." They were such good friends to me, and I was grateful to have someone to drive me. My hands were shaking. And I couldn't stop crying. I couldn't concentrate on anything else except that look of love for me in Mackenzie's ocean blue eyes. I wondered if our lingering goodbye earlier that morning would be the last time I ever saw that recognition that tenderness in those eyes. Becca and Tim tried to bolster my spirits.

I knew Becca had asked all the right questions. Over and over I asked her the details. She patiently answered. She knew how much I loved Mackenzie. We had spent a lot of time together...the three of us. And Becca was my friend and confidante. She knew all about the deepening romance we had woven. All the sweet surprises...all the love that had motivated them. Mackenzie's picture was in that pewter frame Becca had given me. In a prominent place. She was

everywhere in my life in a prominent place. Becca
knew all that.

It worried me that she kept saying we had to hurry. And we
did hurry. Tim drove like we were going to a fire. He did have
experience. But I was glad. I ached to be with her. But this
time it felt so different. I could hardly breathe. Tears seemed
to spring from my soul. And wring life from my own heart.
She was my heart, and I had to be with her. I had to at least try
to help her somehow.

EIGHTEEN: Our Vigil

It was a good thing that Becca was a nurse. She prepared me for the worst-case scenario, the best outcome, and everything in between. I wouldn't accept the worst one…the one where Mackenzie might die on the flight to the hospital. My mind raced along just like the car as it sped towards the city. What would I do if this woman who had become such an integral part of my life were to…die? I could barely think the word "die", and I refused to say it out loud. But a head injury. She could be in a coma for a long time.

I thought myself through all those scenarios. If she was in a coma, I would wait. I would simply hold her hand and wait. I wouldn't leave her side. I had only thrown a change of clothes in my duffel bag. That would have to suffice. I thought about my animals and Mackenzie's dog, Mitch…and her seven horses. We would have to take care of all of them until she regained consciousness and got out of the hospital. Becca and Tim were so good to me to scoop me up and drive me all the way to Atlanta. The trip seemed to take forever. I wanted desperately to see Mackenzie. Just to see for myself that she was still alive would do my wounded heart good.

Just before we pulled into the hospital parking lot, Becca thought of something to ask me. "Do you have a legal power of attorney for Mac?" She asked, referring to the issue that was about to confront us.

"No…we never even thought…" I said, feeling irresponsible and unprepared for all of this. I felt guilty. No one thinks this sort of thing will happen to them. Accidents are what happen to other people. I came from the business world. I should have known better. I should have covered all the bases. Especially in light of the fact that Mackenzie had a dangerous job.

"Don't worry, Sandy…" Becca forced a smile and said, "Hospitals are my world, remember? We'll get you in there if we hafta sneak you in on a gurney." She then told me something I'd never expected. She told me to lie. "Say you're her sister. They'll let you in." She seemed sure as she spoke.

"Mackenzie's mother?" I asked without finishing the sentence. Becca understood what I was asking.

"She's been notified…probably on her way, too." This promised to be a nightmare. We had met before, but she didn't like me. Mackenzie had tried, but parents are far too difficult to train. "I know these things from my job." Becca continued. "This is a big city, yes, and hopefully they are more aware of these sorts of relationships here. But since you're technically not next of kin…"

"Thanks, Becca." I replied. Inside I was kicking myself for not thinking to put something on paper. I was closer to Mackenzie than anyone else alive. Yet here I was preparing to lie just so that I could be by her side in a crisis. A simple piece of paper giving me power of attorney for health care in the event that she became incapacitated and unable to make decisions herself would have given me the right by law to not only be there but to decide what should or shouldn't be done with respect to her care. Now all those things would be decided by her mother. I wondered how she was going to treat me. Her drive was the longer one since she lived in South Georgia. She must be close to Atlanta by now, though. At least I would get to see Mackenzie first.

She was in the recovery room. My heart breathed a sigh. That meant that she was still alive. But she was headed for intensive care since she was in critical condition. The trauma surgeon had closed a three-inch gash in the back of her head and she'd lost a significant quantity of blood. Head wounds bleed a lot. Becca had prepared me. Mackenzie had been placed in a medically induced coma to reduce the swelling of the brain since she'd suffered a fractured skull. But her neck wasn't broken. That was good news.

At first, it didn't look like her. Her head had been shaved. But her soft features were still recognizable. She would have looked like she was sleeping if it were not for the presence of all the tubes in her mouth and nose. I kissed her cheek lightly and willed her eyes to open. They didn't. I wondered if she could hear me as I whispered, "I'm here, honey." I said shakily. "I love you, Mackenzie."

My heart broke to see her like that, but the constant bleeps on the EKG monitor were reassuring to my soul. My heart beat more surely now that I could hear hers on the machine. I grasped her unresponsive hand and held on tight.

"I won't let go of you. And I won't leave you," I promised out loud. "Don't you leave me, honey." I begged. I prayed she could hear me, and I pulled a chair close so I could begin my vigil.

There was a shunt in her head to drain the fluid. It would reduce the pressure that had built up inside her skull. As it dripped the brownish cellular fluid, I watched it fall. It looked nasty. But I decided it was glorious, since it was helping her. The first few days after a head injury were crucial. Everything had been done to help her body help itself. All we could do was to wait and to pray. I was here doing both.

"Your mother is here." The nurse announced. I wondered how my mother could know and have arrived. Then I remembered that I was posing as Mackenzie's sister.

Beverly Coleman brushed past me and kissed her daughter's cheek as she whispered, "My baby. Mama's here, baby." Tears streamed down her stoic face but she wiped them resolutely away and quizzed me. "What have the doctors told you?"

I explained everything I had been told about her injury, the surgery, the medications, the shunt, the coma, and her condition. She hung on my every word. When I finished, she said, "Thank you, Sandy...You may go, now," she spoke coldly. She must have known that I didn't want to go anywhere. I bristled at the thought that she was telling me to go. I opened my mouth to object. But then I remembered what Becca had said about "next of kin" so I decided to tread lightly.

"Thank you, but I want to stay." I replied.

Beverly Coleman straightened up and cut through me with her words. "I want you to leave." She declared. "NOW!" Eyes of steel added emphasis to her words.

"Why?" I asked. It was all I could muster as I unsuccessfully fought back the tears.

"Because I'm here, now." She said flatly. "And you don't belong." She added as she pointed towards the thick recovery room door. "Next of kin only." Tears seemed to spring from the cut she had delivered to my heart.

The nurse looked confused. She was starting to put two and two together and figure out that I wasn't Mackenzie's sister, as I had pretended. I decided that I'd better leave before it got ugly in there. I left Mackenzie's side only a matter of minutes after vowing to her that I would stay. But I had no choice. My heart was ripping inside my chest.

Becca and Tim saw the pain on my face as I approached them in the waiting room. Their eyes begged. Becca brushed tears away from her cherub cheeks. She really was an angel, and I thanked God they were here. At least I didn't have to sit out here alone.

"What happened, honey?" Becca asked as she put her arm around me for comfort.

"Her mom kicked me out." I managed to say despite the flood of tears that garbled my words.

"Just let her be…for a while." Becca admonished. "Give her time." She added. "It'll be all right." I was Humpty Dumpty and she was trying as hard as she could to piece me back together again. And it wasn't working.

Tim tried too. "She'll let you in."

"But what if she wakes up and I'm not there? I promised her…" I whimpered.

"If she heard you promise," Becca reasoned, "Then she also heard her mama tell you to leave." Her experience showed. "And she can't wake up…not for a while."

I remembered the medication that kept her in a coma. Like a prisoner in a spider's web, she was trapped there…and she was also unconscious. She was alive, but none of us knew for how long.

"She said I don't belong." I complained.

"You most certainly DO belong!" Becca and Tim said in unison. "More than anyone..." Becca added. "And I will talk to Beverly...she likes me, and I know how." She went on to explain how family members lose all sense of logic at times like these. And they are protective and territorial and possessive. I understood. I felt that way about Mackenzie, too. But I wasn't technically 'next of kin'. I hated that part. Becca's words were comforting. Her promise to try and talk sense into Mrs. Coleman helped, too.

Becca was a good friend. She was also a skilled mediator, and Beverly liked her. They had met at a barbeque at Mackenzie's house during the summer that had just passed. Becca's bread-baking recipes had been common ground. Now only Becca seemed to know the secret recipe for granting me entrance to the Intensive Care Unit that would soon hold the love of my life.

When they wheeled the bed by the window en route towards Intensive Care, I wanted to burst through the door. I wanted to push her mother away. I did belong. But she was Mackenzie's mother. They loved each other...I knew that.

Mackenzie arrived at the Intensive Care Unit. We followed at a distance like groupies at a concert. The nurse asked Mrs. Coleman to wait outside while they got her daughter situated. That gave Becca time to act.

I couldn't hear the exchange of words. But I soon found out it had been unsuccessful. Relegated to the waiting room, I vowed that if my dear Mackenzie lived, we would sign those papers one day. This wasn't remotely where I belonged. It was so unfair. Sure her mother had given birth to the woman. I'd fulfilled her dreams. She'd told me as much. Over and over again. But there I sat. On the outside in a plastic chair. Like a nobody. I was on a pedestal in Mackenzie's mind. I knew that. But she was unconscious...in a coma. I buried my face in my hands and cried. Prayed. Begged God to keep my love alive.

I ached. I longed to touch Mackenzie's face…to kiss her soft cheek again and again. I remembered running my fingers through her sleek black hair. It was gone now…shaved away along with my sense of security. I wanted to be there when she woke up. But I knew it would be a while. The medicine insured that. At least I was right outside her room. Maybe her mother would at least tell us if she regained consciousness. It wouldn't be for a while though. The medicine did its work silently. And the shunt steadily diverted the fluid that her body had sent to the site of the injury. The fluid dripped. The hours kept pace…a snail's pace.

Tim went home to feed all of our animals. Becca stayed there with me. Thank God. I would have lost my mind being banished to the waiting room if Becca had not been there to keep me company. We sat in silence much of the time. Neither of us read anything. We could think of nothing else except Mackenzie. We talked about the things that really matter in life. Those we love. Everything else instantly pales to insignificance at times like this. Bills, and food and the petty day-to-day details seem to vanish when a life hangs in the balance. I vowed to remember that always after this. The tyranny of the trivial would never be allowed to own me again. Not even for an instant.

"Will you go in…sit with her for a while?" Beverly asked me. Her voice couldn't have sounded sweeter to me.

"Of course. Thank you…thank you…" I replied with tears of gratitude spilling from the well of my heart and eyes. Becca had gotten through to her, after all. They had talked several times during the two days of agony I had spent in the anonymity of the waiting room. More had taken place during those exchanges than I knew. I wanted to kiss Becca.

My love looked asleep. The force of the blow to her head had blackened both her eyes and she looked like a sleeping raccoon. I carefully kissed her cheek and begged her to open her eyes. "I'm back, honey." I whispered. "Wake up, Mackenzie, please…" I touched her face softly with my lips as I spoke. "Your mama let me back in. You can thank Becca for that when you wake up."

God how I did love this woman. My heart tried to turn itself inside and out just to will her well. I would easily have given my life then and there for her. Or I would willingly lie down to take her place in that world of fog. If it would bring her back. But all I could do was wait. And hope.

Her mother was back. "The doctors stopped the medicine that has been keeping her in a coma," she informed me. "So maybe she'll wake up soon."

"Did they say how long?" I asked and dared to make eye contact. I was afraid she would kick me to the curb again. She didn't. I was grateful.

"Nobody knows." She told me what I already suspected.

Days turned into weeks. Beverly softened. She warmed to me. Becca had explained. Plus she had to see firsthand how much I loved her daughter. We took turns sitting in the room with her. I tried to be considerate. She seemed to notice that. Mackenzie's condition had been upgraded and she was no longer in Intensive Care. But she still didn't wake up. We hoped. All of us. Her fan club. We were all on a vigil. Becca, Beverly, and I. One of us was always there. Beverly had rented us a hotel room nearby with two big beds. I never left the hospital. My promise. I showered in her little bathroom every other day or so. Becca had gotten Tim to bring me things from home…deodorant, shampoo, and more clothes. Many of Mackenzie's horseshoeing clients visited. They brought flowers, food, and well wishes. I started a guest book so she would know they had been there and be able to thank them one day for making the journey. She meant so much. To so many people. If she only knew. I told her everything. I relished the long nights alone with her. Just me. Like before, only profoundly different. At least I had this time alone with her.

The nurses rolled her each day so she wouldn't get bedsores. They cleaned her head wound. They bathed her as I had done so many times. But this wasn't the same. Her hair was becoming jet-black stubbles and I wondered how long it would get before she woke up from the coma. I remembered how

silky her ebony soft hair had felt on the bare skin of
my chest as she slept there. I longed for that feeling of
closeness again and for the life that we had shared. Late at
night, I sometimes carefully slid the covers back and climbed
into her bed and held her while she slept. If she woke up I
wanted it to be in my arms. Once a nurse came in to check on
Mackenzie. Afterwards, she pulled the blanket back over us
both. She knew the love we shared. But I was careful not to
be found that way by her mother in the morning. That would
be too much.

More than three weeks had passed. Twenty-four days to be
exact. I had never left her side…except to go to the bathroom.
Her room was mine. As it should be. I ate here, I slept here. I
lived here. With her. Where I belonged. I wondered about
my crops, but I didn't care if they all shriveled up and died. As
long as she didn't. And I knew Becca and Tim were looking
after things. Becca had needed to go back to work. Her
nursing job. Only Beverly and I stood vigil. And at night,
when she left for the hotel, I pushed the cot as close to the bed
as I could. If I positioned it just right, I could hold her hand.
While we both slept. She was in some sort of dreamland all
her own. But I was there holding on. Then, in the middle of
the night…one night…she squeezed my hand! SHE
SQUEEZED MY HAND! I bolted up like a powerful missile.
Had I imagined it? Had I dreamed it?

"Mackenzie?!?" I called out for her as I fumbled for the light
and searched her face for recognition. "You awake, honey?" I
asked. My eyes darted as they had right after that first
kiss…studying the face I loved more than anything in this
world. They studied her for movement. The soft light fell on
her still-closed eyelids. I kissed them both and begged her to
wake up. Then I felt it. It was unmistakable this time. She
squeezed my hand. Hard. Then she coughed and her sweet
lips parted.

"Hey," she said, with a raspy Rip Van Winkle voice. It was the
sweetest sound I think I have ever heard. I will never, as long
as I live forget the timber of her lovely voice as she spoke. At
long last, she had spoken.

Her eyelids opened and her blue eyes emerged. I kissed her mouth and my tears rained down on us both. She kissed me back for the first time in almost a month. The longest month of my life. Her mouth was dry and she swallowed and licked her lips. She coughed again. I sighed and kissed her cheek. I closed my eyes and thanked God for this moment.

"What happened?" She asked.

"You got kicked in the head by a horse." I explained. "You're in the hospital...but you're gonna be o.k." Relief spilled out along with a new type of tears. Then I strained to see that look in her blue eyes. That look of love that is only for me. Her eyes were open. Finally. But something was wrong. There was no recognition. No love pouring out from them. I moved closer and she spoke.

"Why is it so dark in here?" She asked. "Is it nighttime?" As she moved she held her head. "My head hurts." That was no surprise.

"Here, I'll turn on the big light." I obliged. "But it's gonna hurt your eyes," I warned. But when I turned the bright overhead light on, Mackenzie did not so much as blink.

"Where are you?" She screamed.

"I'm right here, honey." I said as I kissed her. She held me close then pushed me back a little and blinked. She squinted. And blinked again. She was looking right at me. But nothing. I realized what was happening. Mackenzie was BLIND! She was alive and she was even awake. But she was blind. I was sure of it.

NINTEEN: Awareness

"Sandy," she said carefully, "will you turn on a light in here please?"

"It is on, honey." I said dejectedly. "You can't see me?" I answered and asked at the same time. I already knew the ugly truth she was just now beginning to realize. The blow to her head had been a bad one. Steel and strength meeting flesh and bone. Her head.

Mackenzie began to weep. So did I. I held her and told her how much I'd missed her. Missed us. I told her I'd never left her side. I told her how many days we had been in the hospital. She asked about her mother and Mitch...and her horses. And mine. I thanked her for waking up.

"I'm sorry." She sighed.

"For what?" I said with astonishment. "For getting kicked?" That was silly. She obviously didn't want that to have happened.

"For making you worry." She finished her sentence.

"You didn't mean it, baby." I said as I brushed away tears from both of our faces. I tried to tell her she would be okay, but I had absolutely no idea what I was even saying. Prying myself away, I told her I was going to go let the medical personnel know that she was awake.

"No, don't leave me..." she begged. "It's so dark."

"I won't go, honey." I promised, firmly gripping her hand. "I can buzz the nurse with this." The buzzer that she couldn't see sat nearby on the bed. Within a few seconds, the nurse burst into the room.

"What happened?" She asked as she called to her patient. "You awake, honey?" She asked as she used the term of endearment that I thought was only mine.

"Yep...I am." Mackenzie replied and managed a weak smile. The nurse noted the time. It was three-twenty in the morning.

"But I can't see a thing." She added the bad news. Good news, bad news.

The nurse tried to reassure her as she took her vital signs. "Well, the blindness might only be temporary." She noted. "Happens." Systematically, she took Mackenzie's temperature. Then her blood pressure and heart rate. All were within normal limits. "Can you see anything…shapes, colors, light, anything?" She quizzed Mackenzie as she shined a penlight into each eye. Mackenzie was oblivious that a bright little light was aimed directly into her eye from only a few inches away. Tears slipped steadily out of her eyes and down her face.

I slipped her a tissue as the nurse spoke again. "Just glad to have you back." She adjusted the covers. "You got kicked by a horse, I heard…and you were out for a while as a result." The nurse must've thought that Mackenzie was blind and I was a deaf mute. "I need to report," she announced her departure. "The doctor will be in to see you."

The horse had kicked her near her left ear. The sutures had been removed, and the wound was almost completely healed. I touched the new pink skin and accidentally startled her since she couldn't see my hand as it approached her head.

"Sorry, honey." I apologized. "Does this hurt?" I asked as I bent over and lightly kissed the scar.

"Not really." She rustled. "But I still have a whale of a headache." She admitted and rubbed the other side of her head. "How do you like my haircut?" She looked blankly in my direction and asked.

"You look beautiful." I said firmly…remembering at that instant that I had a lock of her sleek black hair at home in an alabaster keepsake box. But here we both were. In the hospital in Atlanta staring at the possibility of blindness. We discussed it all calmly, rationally, and together. At least she remembered me and we had 'us' back. We held each other close while I was sitting on the edge of her bed.

"Sandy, I need you now, more than you know." She said, with the softness that was only for me. I could only hear it in her voice. Her eyes were expressionless blue caverns that moved around the room with abandon. She searched to see, but came up empty. The blackness of the room was marked by the realization that she might never see light or color...or my face again. Much less a horse's foot. Her career. She had not said anything about any of that, but I knew her. She had to be sifting through all those thoughts.

"I'm sticking with you...no matter what." I said as I held her close and squeezed her hand. "You do know that?" I asked even though I knew she was fully aware of my loyalty.

"Yeah," she said as she kissed my cheek. "I know that."

"I better call your mom." I remembered. Even though it was the middle of the night, I knew she would want to know that Mackenzie was conscious. Reaching for the phone, I dialed the phone number for the motel. "Room 137 please," I requested the operator. Only then did I piece together what I would say.

"Hello, what's wrong?" She asked. When you are awakened in the night, you automatically assume the worst. Especially when your daughter is in a coma.

"Nothing's wrong...Mackenzie woke up!" I proclaimed happily. "She's okay except she can't see." Her mom didn't react to the blindness.

"I'll be right there." Was all she said before she hung up. That reminded me of the way Mackenzie would do the same thing when she wanted to hurry to be with me. I knew how she must feel.

"Where is she...my mom?" Mackenzie asked.

"In a motel...nearby." I informed her.

"How long have I been out?" She asked as she fumbled with her hospital gown.

"Twenty-five days." I replied.

"Wow, no wonder my head hurts." She said and her eyes darted even though she couldn't see. She was processing it all. And rubbing the uninjured side of her head. "This Sinead O'Connor look must be ridiculous." She added.

"Nah…actually, it's really sexy." I said with a smile.

"I can hear your smile," she smiled too. "Wish I could see it," she said as she traced the outline of my lips that had been frozen in a smile since she woke up. "You are beautiful, I can see that even if I'm blind forever." She said as a tear rivered its way down to her cheek. Then she kissed me deeply. My baby was back.

"Can I do something?" She asked as she investigated my face. With both hands she explored the contours of my face, my eyes, and the outline of my jaw. She ran her hands through my hair. God how I'd missed this. And I was grateful that she didn't have amnesia from the injury. What if she'd awakened and I was a stranger to her? That would have killed me. Then she used my hair to pull my mouth to hers. She kissed me deeply until the doctor interrupted.

"So you're awake, I see." He said and introduced himself as he approached the other side of her bed. Poor choice of words. But she was awake. Adjusting the bed so Mackenzie was more upright, he took her other hand. Her head turned towards him. "I'm going to do a few tests." He said. He used a little rubber mallet to check her reflexes. "All normal." He proclaimed.

"I'm blind, Doc." Mackenzie said succinctly.

"I heard…but that may be a temporary result of the hematoma you developed after your cranial fracture." He said in doctor speak. "I'm shining a light in your right eye…can you see anything…anything at all?" He asked. She shook her head to say, "No." The same result with the other eye. Then he asked her routine questions…what her name was…where she was…what she did for a living…what my name was. She answered everything perfectly. When he asked her what day it was, she said, "I have no idea….but if I've been out twenty-five days that would make this….September something." She at least knew what month it must be. That was enough for the doctor. But she added. "I don't remember getting kicked…. I don't even remember where I was."

"That is very common…almost protective." The doctor explained. "Your brain spares you the unpleasant by blanking out a period of time before the injury." As he was speaking, Mackenzie's mother burst into the room. I backed away from the bed to make room for Beverley.

"Baby, you're awake." She said with tears welling up in her brown eyes. Tears of joy and tears of relief. She cradled Mackenzie's face in her hands and kissed her gently on her forehead. "Do you hurt, Mac?" She asked, shortening the name she'd bestowed upon her daughter at birth.

"Headache." She grimaced. "Plus, I can't see." She informed her mother of her own blindness. Another tear slipped from the blank blue cavern of an eye. With that, Beverly turned to face the nodding doctor.

"Mrs. Coleman, we have done preliminary neurological tests on your daughter," the doctor explained. "But we'll need to do more." The doctor moved around the bed joining Beverly on the other side. Eclipsing my view. He addressed her and explained everything…to her…and to Mackenzie. Leaving me totally out. Their little conference didn't include me. Becca had made progress with Beverly. But I was still not a family member in any one's eyes. This needed to change. But I bit my tongue. The last thing Mackenzie needed right now was a verbal altercation between the two women she loved.

"Becca!" I gasped. "I should call…" I said as I reached for the phone and dialed the number from memory. She answered on the second ring. The news of Mackenzie's awakening was a welcomed relief. But she sensed something in my voice and asked, "What's wrong?"

"She can't see." I said softly cupping the phone against my face and turning to face the window…away from Mackenzie. "They're doing tests…but everything else neurologically is okay so far…" I said. She had questions. I answered as much as I knew to tell her and promised to tell Mackenzie that she and Tim love her very much and would drive up to visit. All of our animals were fat and sassy. It was good to hear the hope in Becca's voice once again. She could always be counted on for that. What a dear friend she'd become to us both.

Tests and more tests. The doctors scurried about and spoke to each other and to the nurses in whispers. Mackenzie's mother was holding her hand, so I had slipped out to use the bathroom. The little hospital room bathroom. As I was drying my hands I heard Mackenzie scream, "Where is she?" She cried out frantically. "Sandy?" She called as she slid from the bed and stood. Using her right hand she ripped the IV out of her arm and flailed forward with her arms reaching for me...reaching everywhere in hopes that I was nearby. Her knees buckled.

"I'm here." I answered as I helped her to her feet. Then she pushed me away and vomited.

She groaned and leaned over wrenching. Her mother was on the other side of her now...and so was the nurse. "You're weak, baby...let's get you back in bed." Beverly said. The nurse retrieved the reeling IV. None of us could imagine how weak she must have felt when she tried to stand. All that time in a coma. And no solid food. Sure she had a feeding tube, but that wasn't the same as solid food. We cleaned her up, and she frowned. She wanted to know why I left her when I promised I never would.

"I want you here...for everything, unless you tell me..." She hugged me as she pleaded. Her mother looked on with arms crossed in front of her body.

"Well, they all have to leave now...and so do you." The nurse demanded. "Your doctors have ordered tests."

"NO!" Mackenzie bellowed. "No tests...not unless you go with me." She added. Finally, someone realized that I belonged with this woman. "Nurse?" She called out again. It was hard to look authoritative when you glared off in the wrong direction. But the nurse heard.

"Let's get you going." The nurse said as she wheeled the wheelchair up to the side of the bed.

"Not so fast," Mackenzie said with a frown on her face and in her voice. "Not until I sign one of those papers."

"What papers?" The nurse asked. She'd heard our entire exchange. Certainly she knew what Mackenzie meant.

"A paper that gives Sandy rights…you know…" As she spoke, Mackenzie pulled me closer legitimizing my importance in this room and in her life. Her mother groaned.

"Power of Attorney?" The nurse had a synapse.

"Yes, please." Mackenzie requested. As she spoke she smiled and looked towards me even though she couldn't see. She stroked my hand as if I were injured. Actually, I had been injured…by being left out. That seemed to be changing. Now that Mackenzie was conscious, everything was changing.

The nurse returned with the paper. "Here's the form…" she alerted Mackenzie to the paper on the clipboard that was being placed in her lap. "And here's a pen."

"Will you read it to me, please?" She asked the nurse. "Read every word, so no one can say I was blind and had no idea what I was signing."

As the nurse read every word, every delicious word, Mackenzie listened intently. And her mother fumed in the corner like a jealous child. Her signature had to be witnessed by two people. And Beverly refused to sign. That opened up a chasm between mother and daughter. I had never before seen Mackenzie angry. "Get me another nurse then…if my mother doesn't care about what I want!" She demanded.

Even though I hated to see her upset, I knew it was for a good cause. And I was thankful that it had been her idea and at her initiation…not mine. "Do I hafta hit everybody else in the head here to get you people to realize what this woman means to me?" She implored anyone within earshot. Then she spelled it out. She told everyone, including her pouting mother, that she was in love with me…how I made her feel wanted and needed…and alive. I found it almost hard to breathe on the pedestal she'd just placed me upon.

"NOW…where do I sign this damn thing?" She asked as she felt the paper as if it were Braille. I held back not wanting to take control or to be accused of manipulating Mackenzie.

"Right here." The second nurse pointed the pen in the right direction.

Mackenzie signed the form and demanded a copy for the hospital, one for me, and one for herself. She smiled triumphantly. "Now, I'll be happy to go for tests…as long as this woman goes with me." She boldly held my hand. My heart wanted to jump right out of my chest. And Beverly wanted to crawl into the woodwork. I felt bad for her. But the form did have her daughter's signature on it. And the two nurses had witnessed it, as well. She was probably feeling the same helplessness I felt out in the Intensive Care Unit's waiting room. Parents have a hard time letting go. Especially when a relationship is unconventional like ours.

I felt the chasm widen between Mackenzie and her mother. Even though I tried to include her. After all, she had asked me to sit with her daughter. And she was Mackenzie's mother. She deserved to be there. But now, so did I. On paper. I accompanied Mackenzie to each and every test. When the doctors spoke, they included me. We were all involved. Mackenzie had become a force to be reckoned with.

"Just because I'm blind, don't think I'm a wimp!" She had said to her mother once. We all laughed out loud at that thought. And it brought us all closer emotionally as we hugged her tightly while we laughed.

I was falling more and more and more in love with Mackenzie with every tick of the clock on her hospital room wall. Each and every day, I held her hand and accompanied her for whatever testing the doctors ordered. She started to feel like a guinea pig after a while. And she was getting restless. But she still saw only darkness…interminable unyielding darkness that only the blind can comprehend. Only in her dreams could she see. Often she would awaken softly crying to herself when she realized that it was only a dream. I would climb in the bed and hold her while she cried.

Her hair was growing back quite well. But the scar itched constantly…a nagging and ragged reminder of the source of her blindness. It was purple and tender, but it seemed to be healing properly. Twice a day, I rubbed Vitamin E oil on it to keep it supple and to help it heal. She thought it was funny that I was worried about a scar since her hair was rapidly shielding it from anyone's view. If I could erase it altogether I would have. Pampering her came naturally to me. Her mother had gone home to South Georgia. When it came time for Mackenzie to go home, she would return.

We were growing more and more discouraged about the possibility of her sight returning. All the tests only confirmed what we already knew. The part of her brain that enables vision had been severely bruised and damaged by the horse's kick.

"Doc," she blurted out one day during another fruitless test. "I wanna go home."

"All right, Mackenzie." The doctor agreed. "But after you complete your occupational therapy." When he stood to leave, he asked if he could talk with me in private. She agreed as long as we promised we weren't making fun of her hair.

"I know Mackenzie has your support." He gave me credit. "But I'd like her to have counseling…here and maybe follow-up at home." He went on to explain that blindness is difficult and we agreed counseling would be a good idea…in addition to the occupational therapy. She had to learn to walk with a cane. And she had to begin to process the fact that she would be living out her life in the dark.

When I re-entered her room, I explained what the doctor wanted. She seemed relieved to know that all he wanted was for her to see a shrink. "I guess this is a lot to get used to." She spoke a mouthful. "It really sucks…and I can't shoe horses…not like this."

I knew we could do it together. All that time of waiting for her eyes to open had given me the courage to do just about anything. Anything life threw my way. Even though we both knew that shoeing horses was a thing of the past, I was certain we could find a way through this together.

Occupational therapy was an enigma. Or a misnomer. Now that she was blind, Mackenzie had no occupation. But she needed to learn to deal with all the adjustments that blindness presented. Going to the bathroom, bathing, grocery shopping, and even pouring a glass of water all posed their own difficulties. And so did walking. Until therapy, I'd held her arm…escorting her during our walks around the hospital. We both adored parading around in public holding onto each other. But she needed to walk on her own…using a cane. Proof she had a 'disability.' When the therapist handed her the cane, she started to cry. I held her and reminded her that she was alive. Being blind wasn't as bad as losing her.

"Just give me a minute." She pulled in air, and wiped her tears away resolutely. "It's just I never pictured one of these for me." She added. I was glad we were going to talk with that counselor. We could both use some help dealing with this. My feelings of helplessness grew. But so did my determination to hurdle every obstacle that reared its ugly head. We had forged a life together. This could only be considered a bump in that road. A big bump.

I wanted to help her when she fumbled and banged into things. But the therapist reminded me. Independence is crucial for a blind person. Even though I had put my life on hold for her, she did need to learn to walk around by herself. Mackenzie tried to walk too fast. Then she held back and walked like she was afraid of what lay ahead. In some ways we both were. But we both longed to be at home. Alone. Even though we faced a huge hurdle, we wanted to get on with it.

It had been months since either of us had stepped out of the hospital. When we talked about home, our conversations centered on our animals. Even though we knew that Becca and Tim were taking care of things, we missed our 'kids.' Mackenzie's mother had agreed to pick us up from the hospital and drive us home. She would stay on for a few days. Long enough to see that we were situated there. She offered to stay long-term. Mackenzie denied. "No offense, Mama." She'd replied. "But being alone with Sandy is what I really need." So she settled for being our chauffeur. The thought of Mackenzie's house and of her bed made me weak. All those pillows. We could fall asleep in each other's arms just like we had done before this disruption happened.

"Come here." Mackenzie whispered in the darkness. So I left my little cot and climbed into the hospital bed with her. She pulled the blankets over us both and we fell into the deep sleep that profound comfort affords. The nurse awakened us with breakfast early. I sat on the bed and started to feed her as I'd been doing. Then I remembered. So did Mackenzie.

"Let me try." She said as she reached for the fork. "Gimme some bearings, please."

"Your eggs are at high noon." I began. "Bacon cuts the plate in half from three o'clock to nine o'clock...three strips." A clock had become important again for us. "Orange slices at four...and cottage cheese at eight." She ate aggressively and I knew her appetite was a good sign. When she dropped food onto herself, I wasn't sure what to do. Maybe I could ask the counselor we were seeing later in the day.

"When we get home, let's stay in bed all day." I teased her and kissed the side of her face. Touching her shoulder en route to kissing her had been my early warning system. That way I could kiss her without frightening her in the process.

"When are they gonna let me out of here?" She asked in between bites.

"After the counselor." I reminded her of our appointment after breakfast. "But I promise to have you home in bed naked before the sun sets."

"I can hardly wait." She said with a smile. "What should I say to the counselor?"

"Just tell her how you feel." I replied. "We both will. But don't tell her our plan to be in bed naked before the sun sets. That's our little secret."

"Probably a good idea." She agreed. "Better not let my mom in on that little tidbit either." She added something I had forgotten about. Mackenzie's mother would be staying in the house. While we were in bed in the master bedroom. And we would have to be quiet for her sake. For the first time ever in our relationship. Quiet passion that we wanted desperately to unleash.

The counselor was helpful. But it was awkward. She tried to ask us how we felt about this, how we would deal with that. It was hard to say how we would deal with every little detail of our future. In some ways, this was no different than any other of life's issues. All we could do was to promise to work through problems as they arose. For better or for worse. We had not exchanged the vows, but we were no less committed to each other. The counselor gave us the name and number of one of her colleagues. And she promised us we would need to talk with the counselor once we settled in at home. "This issue will bring you close…or it will rip you apart…I guarantee that." She promised. Cheery lady. But I knew she was right. We loved each other though. She could tell. "Talk…make sure you say how you feel…if you keep things in it'll make this harder." She left us with that thought and wished us well. Her job must be a tough one. Ours was life…even tougher at this point.

Beverly arrived as planned. Mackenzie did a pretty good job with the cane. Her nurses gathered around and said their goodbyes. We had grown fond of them. Most of them understood our relationship. The ones that didn't approve kept their distance.

As we emerged from the hospital, the sunlight flooded our faces. Mackenzie stopped. "Sunshine." Mackenzie noticed. "Weird, for it to be so dark." She said as she paused to enjoy the warmth. Her mom and I exchanged knowing sympathetic looks. She had the same kind look in her eyes even though they were brown. And her olive skin was just like Mackenzie's. Both were beautiful women. As we wound our way to the car, I noticed their similarities. And I wondered what it would be like to have Beverly in "our house."

At least we were finally leaving the hospital.
Mackenzie might have been blinded by this accident. But she was alive. And we were on our way home. We were on our way back to try and pick up where we had left off. Our idyllic life was going to be different. Things had changed for us in the blink of an eye. By the kick of a horse.

Life can be like that. But so much had changed for me over the last two years. My life was hardly recognizable in comparison to the previous one I had lived in the city. Now Mackenzie faced monumental adjustments in hers. In ours. I had initiated the changes in my life. She had not willed or caused these changes that we were driving towards. Intended or not, such is life. And I knew our bond was a good one. I reached for her hand beside the passenger's seat. It was there. Her tight grip told me she was ready to bravely face it all with me.

TWENTY: Homecoming

We were finally on our way home. All three of us were nervous. But we were clearly breathing a collective sigh of relief to be headed home with Mackenzie.

"How about some real food, girls?" Beverly asked. She seemed eager to promote a positive mood for this day.

"Sounds good, Mom." Mackenzie replied. Anyone would be sick of hospital food by now. Especially someone who could cook as well as she could. "Aren't we near the Galleria?" She asked. One of her favorite restaurants was there. The Silver Spoon Restaurant was our unanimous choice. "Time to try out my new skills." Mackenzie added. This was only the beginning of an entirely new world for her. She seemed so brave to me. Normally confident and assertive, I was scared to death about this. And I could see.

People gave Mackenzie strange looks. And they spoke louder to her. "I'm blind, not deaf." She reminded the waitress. For some reason people seemed to feel compelled to raise their voices when addressing her. When she walked, she fumbled with the cane, but refused our help. We all ate pasta and shared a bottle of Chardonnay. There was a festive air about this meal. I even sensed that Beverly was beginning to like me. She couldn't deny my loyalty to her daughter since I had not left Mackenzie's side during the extended hospital stay.

"I bet your crops are coming along." Mackenzie turned towards me and said. "Corn should be ready..." She deduced. I hoped she was right.

"Thanks to Becca and Tim." I concluded. "This farmer ran off to be a nurse."

"Thanks, Baby." Mackenzie reached for my hand. It meant so much to me. Especially that she called me 'Baby' in front of her mother. And that she reached for and held my hand as a way of legitimizing and emphasizing our relationship. For everyone to see. I liked that.

117

Beverly took another bite of her food and added, "Yes, Sandy…you made a tremendous sacrifice." I could hardly believe my ears.

"Your daughter is worth it." I said. Mackenzie squeezed my hand again. Then we all resumed eating in silence. We each digested the meaning of what was happening. Out in public and very privately, Mackenzie and I were together. Even her mother was admitting it. She even seemed to be embracing the idea. We really had come a long way. None of us wanted to linger over the food. Home beckoned.

It felt so good to be headed home. Mackenzie's house had come to feel like my home, as well. Leaves were falling from the trees lining the driveway as we brushed past.

"We're turning into the driveway, Honey." Beverly said alerting Mackenzie as to our arrival.

"Do you hear Mitch?" I asked. The Golden retriever had joined us to serve as our escort down the driveway.

"Yeah…" Mackenzie said wistfully. "I hope he remembers me."

"I'm sure he will." I concluded. "It hasn't been that long….and it looks like he got a bath for this occasion." Becca knew we were coming home today. And it seemed as if she and Tim had pulled out all the stops. There was a banner stretched across the doorway of the house. It read, "Welcome Home Mackenzie!" People were milling around on the porch and out in the front yard. Tim spotted us first and heralded our arrival. He was manning the grill and the smell of barbeque was wafting our way.

"I smell food." Mackenzie stated. "Somebody must be grilling out."

"You are." I said. "You're having a party." I touched her shoulder and kissed her left cheek. Beverly and I informed her that her yard was overflowing with people. Her friends and neighbors were all here to welcome her home. We told her about the banner over the door and the party that was about to happen. It had not seemed like a good idea to frighten her when she stepped from the car cane in hand.

She seemed pleased yet embarrassed. "Hope I don't frighten them." She said in a worried tone. "Do I look presentable?" She asked me.

"You look great!" I said reassuringly. Honestly she did look great. Even though her eyes were vacant and her hair was different, she was still striking. Plus, I knew that every person there was thrilled just to see her. And to have her alive. To welcome her home.

Mitch greeted her first. He whined that excited dog whine that dogs seem to do when they are really really happy to see someone special. And he licked her face. Then one by one, Mackenzie's friends, neighbors, and horseshoeing customers came up to wish her well. They all hugged her tightly and many had even brought presents. All were careful to tell Mackenzie who it was when they approached. Most of her clients were people I didn't recognize. They obviously loved her. And she asked about their horses. We were all overwhelmed with the throng that had swelled in her honor that day. Country music played on the stereo and could be heard in the background through the open windows.

"Becca, where are you?" Mackenzie called out.

"Right here, Sweetie...I'm on my way." Becca replied as she dried her hands and made her way through the crowd to Mackenzie.

"Thank you, Becca. For all this." Mackenzie beamed. "This is quite a shin dig." She said as she grabbed Becca and hugged her tightly. "And where's that teddy bear of a husband of yours?" She said reaching out for Tim.

"Here I am, Mac." Tim announced. Mackenzie welcomed him into the dual embrace.

"Thank you...both." She said and she kissed each of them on a smiling cheek. "You two...you are true friends..." She began as a tear slipped from each eye and her voice quivered. "You cooked all this up and you've been taking care of everything

here…all my animals…all this time." Sincerity
flavored her words.

"You're welcome." They said in unison. "You'd have done
the same for us." Becca added. It was true. That was
something I'd suddenly come to appreciate about life in a small
town. Or life in the South. Or both. People here not only
knew their neighbors, but they rallied around each other in
times of need. I'd lived in the same house in the same
neighborhood in Ohio for twenty years before moving away to
come to Georgia. Yet I had only known five of my neighbors.
People had weathered diversity just down the street and I never
even knew their names. I'd been through some tough times
there, too. Alone. I may as well have been a hermit atop a
mountain all by myself. None of my neighbors knew me well.
Nobody offered me support even when I was going through my
divorce. And I'd not expected it. But this was so much better.

As I stood in this yard full of people, people who really cared
for Mackenzie, I was never more certain that this life I had
chosen was a better one. Anonymity is lonely. It has its safety
factor, but human beings need each other. We especially
needed all this support in times such as these. The party
wound to a close. One by one, people said their 'goodbyes' to
Mackenzie. Everyone reminded her that if she needed
anything they'd help. People pitched in to help with the clean
up. But we decided to leave the banner over the door for a
while.

We had enough food left over to feed an army. Barbeque beef
and chicken. Baked beans. Potato salad. But Becca had
cleaned out the fridge. And restocked with creamer and things
she thought we would need upon returning home. She was like
that. We all decided that Becca was a shoe in for sainthood.
Both of them. They had worked their jobs full-time in addition
to taking care of all of our animals all this time. And they had
tended to my crops, as well. I really didn't know how they had
done it all. But you could tell that they were the sort of people
who thrive on giving to other people. Unselfishness is a virtual
transfusion. How I did admire their spirits!

The sun was starting to set by the time everybody had gone. Mitch was curled up by the fireplace and seemed happy to be inside. Embers fell to the bricks. Our energy seemed to crinkle right along with them. Mackenzie had fallen asleep on the couch and it felt good to see her relax at home. But I had a promise to keep. Through the curtains I could see the sun starting to sink below the horizon. I had promised to have her naked in bed with me by the time the sun set on this day.

Beverly had made herself at home in the guest room. I had deposited my duffel bag in Mackenzie's room. Where I knew I belonged. I could hardly wait to slide into that familiar bed. Naked under those crisp sheets with the love of my life at home at last.

"Let's go to bed, Honey." I whispered to Mackenzie and kissed her on the forehead. She woke up instantly and reached for my arm as she stood.

"You won't have to twist my arm on that one." She said wearily. "But I want you…not my cane." She requested with a sigh. I understood. "Goodnight Mom." Mackenzie said searching the room for her mother as we walked. "Thanks for everything." She added.

"Goodnight, baby." Beverly said with that maternal tone. "Sleep tight."

"You too." Mackenzie said as she kissed her mom on the cheek. She held me firmly as we walked eagerly towards her bedroom. We went into the room and I shut and locked the door behind us. That was a first. Never before had we slept with the door shut, much less locked. But Mackenzie's mother was just down the hall. At least we could be alone now. We could be naked now. My body reacted with anticipation. I led Mackenzie to the edge of the bed. She sat down and promptly took charge.

She put both her arms around my waist and pulled me down on top of her. She kissed my neck as I fell happily into her outstretched arms. Peeling off my clothes, she skillfully initiated what I had longed to do.

"I don't need to see you to do this." She whispered as
she nibbled her way around both sides of my neck.
Goosebumps jumped to the surface of my skin. I loved it when
she did all that. And the way she kissed me. I kissed back
with all the seduction I'd kept bottled up inside all those weeks.
It had come back instantly when she took charge of me like
this. I felt weak in her grasp.

"I thought you were sleepy." I giggled between rough hungry
kisses.

"It was all an act." She admitted. "I was breathing hard, but I
wasn't asleep. I was planning all of what I wanted to do to you
once we were alone in this bed." She said playfully as she
began to explore my exposed skin. It warmed to her touch.
The aching that we felt was almost palpable in the room.

"I missed you, Honey." I confessed as I freed her from her
clothes. "God, how I missed this." I whispered, as tears
spilled down my face and onto her skin. She tenderly and
purposely led me to that precious place of relief. Spasms rolled
over my body and I started to scream. But I remembered.
Then I pulled her up to my face. She cupped her arm around
my neck and buried her face in my pillow.

"I love you, Sandy." She whispered what I knew so well by
now. "More and more, I love you." She said as tears fell from
her eyes to mix with mine.

"I love you, too, Mackenzie…more than ever." I reminded her
as I parted her budding hair with both my hands. I kissed her
on the forehead. Then, I rolled over on my side and slid up
under her arm. With my head on her chest, I began caressing
her to the cadence of her beating heart. Her breathing
deepened and she shuddered as I ran my open palm along the
inside of her leg. I knew exactly just how to please her. My
mouth watered at the thought of the taste of her. It had been a
very long time, but the familiar taste had not changed. I made
her want to scream with pleasure.

As her body reveled under my touch then quieted, tears
glistened in the moonlight. I wanted to see her better. So I got

up to light a candle…the Christmas candle I had brought to her house the very first time I'd spent the night here.

"Where'd you go?" She whimpered. "I was just getting started."

"I'll be right back…I'm just lighting a candle." I said to reassure her I had not gone far.

"Workin' up a thirst." She smiled. "Will you get us some wine? I think there's some…" She asked as she pointed towards the kitchen.

We were really at home now. And we were both loving our new freedom and falling back into our routine of lovemaking. "I'll be right back with some," I replied as I threw on her terrycloth bathrobe. Mackenzie stretched out both arms and legs spread eagle on the bed and smiled from ear to ear. In the candlelight she was still the gorgeous woman who had taken my breath away the first time I saw her naked. I wanted more. I couldn't wait to resume our lovemaking. But I was thirsty, too.

I closed the door behind me and made my way to the kitchen. A bottle of chardonnay was ready in the wine rack Mackenzie had made out of used horseshoes. The nightlight was all I needed to find the drawer for the corkscrew. Just as the cork popped noisily from the bottle, I realized that someone else was with me in the moonlit kitchen. Mackenzie's mom was sitting at the kitchen table in her flannel nightgown quietly sipping a cup of hot tea she'd made for herself. I tightened the tie on my bathrobe when I realized she was there. When I turned to head back to bed with the wine bottle and two glasses entwined in my fingers, our eyes met. Neither of us said a word. She knew. I wore the musky scent of her daughter all over me. And I was obviously a woman on a mission for wine and a woman in love. What did she expect?

Mackenzie and I had not been alone in months now. And we were finally at home alone behind closed doors. It was probably more than she'd wanted to consider. So she just sat there drinking her tea in the dark. And Mackenzie lay in her own darkness in her candlelit bedroom. When I returned, I

locked the door back. And I poured us each a glass of
the nectar of the gods. But the wine stems proved too difficult
to handle. So we dispensed with all formalities and drank right
from the bottle. Who cared? We were sharing everything else
anyway. Everything else.

I have never loved or been loved more thoroughly than that
night. Physically, emotionally, spiritually, and sexually. We
drained out every drop of the wine and every drop of love's
store. We stayed awake for hours. It was profound.
Mackenzie may have been blind, but she was definitely not
handicapped in bed. The strength was still there in her arms as
she held me. I fell more in love with her as time fell by the
wayside. I had asked Becca for tulips. She remembered. Just
when she thought we might go to sleep, I held one under
Mackenzie's nose and asked her to smell.

"For me?" She asked as she felt the flowers.

"Tulips…yellow ones just like those ones you got for me that
first date." I answered as I began to stroke her with a petal I'd
plucked. We finally fell asleep amid the petals. I have never
felt more at home in a place. I hoped Mackenzie felt that same
comfort. She held me tightly through what was left of the
night as we slept naked at last in her bed.

We awakened to the smell of bacon frying. Beverly was at
work in the kitchen. Neither of us wanted to emerge from the
nest, but the knock on our door summoned.

"Breakfast, you two." Beverly announced. She really was
trying hard to please.

We donned bathrobes and brushed teeth. Washed hands and
faces. And joined her at the kitchen table. I poured coffee for
us both.

"Sleep well?" She asked us both.

"Yeah…good to be home." Mackenzie smiled and reached for
my hand. The wine cork on the counter and the corkscrew
were still there. Even though Beverly had made breakfast, they
were still undisturbed on the kitchen counter. As Mackenzie's
robe fell open I stretched to fix it. Then I stood to refill our

coffee. When I did, I slipped the cork into the pocket of my robe. And I put the corkscrew back where it belonged. Back where I belonged. I bravely kissed Mackenzie on the cheek. And I didn't even look to see her mother's reaction. She was going to have to deal with this…one way or another.

TWENTY-ONE: The Inevitable

Weeks passed like minutes. Being so close to Mackenzie again felt so good to me. Beverly had stayed long enough. Too long in some respects. Once she was gone we had our privacy back and could run around naked if we wanted. And we did. Except Mackenzie couldn't run anywhere. She memorized where all the furniture was in her house and mine. When we went out anywhere, she navigated with her cane.

Our days were spent tending to my crops and caring for the horses. My mares were both due in the summer and got fat on the rich grass and all the supplements I gave them. Onyx took his job of protecting the herd very seriously and even gave Mitch a healthy kick when he ventured too close to one of them. It didn't hurt the dog, but it did give him a newfound respect for the stallion…and for horses in general. Neither Mackenzie nor I'd ever helped with foaling or spent any appreciable time around baby horses, so in the evenings we read. We would sit by the fire and I would read aloud from one of our growing collection of books on mare care or horse training concepts. Mackenzie would listen intently and occasionally she would ask me to repeat a sentence so she could understand it thoroughly. During the day when I was working at home she would sit on my porch and 'watch.' One day in early November when I took a break from my chores to sit down with her, I noticed them. Tears were steadily yet silently flowing down her strained face.

"What's wrong, Mackenzie?" I asked, as I sat on her lap and hugged her close.

"I feel so useless." She whimpered and cried harder. "I just sit here on this porch and rock in this chair like somebody's old Grandpappy."

"You, my dear, are far from being useless." I said kissing her on her cheek.

"And I miss working…shoeing horses." She said rubbing her hands together. "My calluses are all gone. And I bet my tools and my anvil are all rusty by now." They were, but I didn't tell her that. It had been months since her accident, but the humidity here had taken its toll on things. A thin layer of rust had settled on the anvil just like this gloom that was settling on Mackenzie.

I kissed her and wiped her tears away. "You make me feel needed."

"Yeah, but I bet you weren't counting on supporting me forever." She said continuing to spiral downward as if into a black hole. "I'm never gonna work again.... can't be a blind farrier." She said putting words to the realization that had been responsible for this mood.

"We'll find something else for you to do, Baby." I said trying to be hopeful even though I wasn't at all sure what she could do for work. Being a farrier was all I'd known for her. That was how we had met.

"I'm not a BABY!" She chuffed as she stood and stomped her way into my house.

"Hey, stop it...you know what I meant," I said as I followed her through the open door. "Since when am I not allowed to call you pet nicknames?" I asked with a wounded tone added to my voice.

"Since you called me a baby...don't do that." She fumed. "I don't like feeling this way much less having you call me that out loud."

"But I didn't mean..." I started to say something to explain, but she cut me off.

"I'm nothing more than a helpless baby, waiting around for you to feed me or help me take a bath or comb my hair." She gritted her teeth at the reality.

She was starting to make me mad. But I knew she needed to vent. It had been a long time since her accident and resulting blindness. This was the first time I'd seen her express anger. Her life had been altered in an instant. Who wouldn't be upset? It was all to be expected. But her anger seemed to be directed squarely at me.

"I called you 'Baby' long before your accident, and I do not intend to stop now." I vowed.

"Oh yeah, and just how long do you intend to take care of this baby," She asked. "A few more months, maybe a year?" Tears flew from her lips as she yelled. "And when you get tired of being my nursemaid and find somebody else who isn't an invalid, just what am I supposed to do then?" She screamed in a rage.

"Mackenzie, stop this…you're being ridiculous!" I shouted.

"NO I'M NOT!" She interrupted again. "Look at me…or are you blind, too?" She insisted sarcastically as she waved both arms above her head in anger.

Somehow I had to reassure her. No way was I going to bail on her, but it had to be fear that prompted all this. "I told you in the hospital that we would get through this TOGETHER." I reminded her. "For better or for worse, remember?" I asked… proud of my loyalty.

"No I don't remember!" She said with a bite in her tone of voice. "I'm not married to you." She added words that took my breath away. My heart felt like a vacuum when the reality of what she'd said hit me. I was hurt beyond measure that she would say such a thing. When she found her way into the bathroom, I followed.

"After all I did…stayed with you all that time in the hospital." Tears rained uncontrollably from my eyes and pain seemed to spring from my soul and my spirit.

"Leave me alone!" Mackenzie demanded as she slammed the door in my face. "Can't I even pee in private?" She smirked. I had never seen her this angry…this hateful. Mackenzie had never been mean to anyone in all the time I'd known her. Now she was making up for lost time.

"Fine then, be an ass!" I said and left her alone in the house. I was outside feeding the horses when she reappeared on the porch.

"I wanna go home." She said flatly. "And unfortunately, I'm helpless and can't drive. Take me home and then you can get on with your life since that's what you really want after all." She spit through the tears.

"Don't you dare." I sputtered through the tears. "...tell ME what I WANT!" I hated it when anybody put words in my mouth. Normally, I shrank from fighting. But she was hurting me and making me angrier by the moment. I finished feeding and drove her home in silence. It was not at all what I wanted. Even though it was like ripping a part of me away, I had to oblige her. When my truck came to a stop in her driveway, Mackenzie jumped out, cane in hand.

When I came around to help her, she brushed me off with, "I don't need help...turns out I'm not a helpless baby after all." She said curtly as she began to tick out her way with the cane. She managed to make it all the way to the door without tripping over anything even though her anger had caused her to travel way too fast. Mitch followed her along and pushed his way into the house beside her. "Stop watching me!" She commanded. "GO HOME, and leave me alone." She said as the screen door slammed. "I'm sure you have something better to do than watch over me all the time." She snapped as she slammed the door on her words.

I could no longer fight back the tears. Shell-shocked, I stood there beside my truck for what seemed like a long time. I bawled like the baby I was all the way as I drove towards my empty house. And I worried. How could she do everything alone? Should I go back? How would she care for herself? For months now, I had taken care of her, so she'd not needed to cook. She had not spent one day alone since the accident. What now?

My house felt like a tomb. Unlike the early months of our courtship, she had not left once since we came home from the hospital. I'd grown happily accustomed to Mackenzie. She'd been with me always. Now this. It felt awful. I wanted her back. Since the accident my life had become so entwined with hers. Now all that seemed to have unraveled and I had no idea how to stop it. I kept wondering what she was doing...how she

129

was faring alone. When I could stand it no longer, I
picked up the phone and dialed her number.

When she finally answered, I proclaimed, "I miss you,
Mackenzie." Dial tone. She had hung up without a word. I
wondered how someone so tender and so thoughtful could also
be so mean. It hurt to be without her. And it hurt to remember
all the ways I'd stood beside her only to be treated like this. As
I drifted off to sleep I held her pillow to my face. It smelled
like her. But she wasn't there. I cried softly to myself. Her
absence felt foreign and I wondered if I would ever get used to
it. I also wondered if she would ever be back.

I tried to keep busy over the next few days. All the leather I
owned, saddles, bridles glistened after I massaged the
conditioner into it while muttering about how she
misunderstood. Both of my cats twirled around my legs as I
worked. They probably wondered why I was suddenly talking
to myself. All the horses got a thorough grooming…probably
too hard of a brushing since I was angry. When I broke down I
was brushing Zippy. She seemed to understand in that intuitive
way horses know when something is wrong. When she
mothered me and tried to console me, I knew she would be a
good mama when that time came. I went on several long rides
on the stallion. He enjoyed the attention, but I cried the whole
time…each time. Because I was riding without her. And it felt
all wrong.

Several times I even picked up the phone to dial her number.
But I wouldn't grovel. Not my style. She had hung up on me,
after all. Now the ball rested squarely in her court. All I could
do was wait. Each day as I went about my life, all I could do
was think of Mackenzie. Every nook and cranny of my life
and my house was chock full of reminders of her. Candles.
Love notes. Even the coffee made me think of her. So did
sitting on the porch. And climbing into bed at night. Several
times I took out the alabaster keepsake box and poured over the
contents. Tulips. And that lock of her hair. There was not
anything in my life or my activities or my home that failed to
make me think about Mackenzie. Even my horses. And my
cabin.

Sleep came haltingly. When I slept I dreamed. And she was always there in my dreams. I dreamed we were riding. But then I woke up crying. This was killing me. It hurt right down to the depths of my soul. My spirit was bruised and bleeding. Over and over I dreamed she was calling out for my help and I was pushing her away. She needed me and I wasn't there.

Even though my pride wouldn't allow me to call again, I had to know that she was all right. So I decided to drive by. When I did so there was a new Chevy truck parked there…one with Florida license plates. Her ex-girlfriend lived in Florida. Could it be? I had to know. Jealousy stirred me and reddened my face. But I had to see for myself. It was all I could do not to cry out or lose control all together. Sliding to a stop, I jumped out and ran to the door. My knocking brought this stranger to the door.

"Well hello there, good-looking," she said. "What can we do for you?" She asked as she winked and dried her hair with the towel. This woman definitely fit the stereotype. She stood like a grain-fed Soviet on steroids and I wondered how Mackenzie or anyone for that matter could be attracted to this. And then my heart stopped. Mackenzie approached the door clad only in a towel. "Who is it?" Was all I heard her say before I turned on my heels and left without a word. Why had I gone there? Just to break my own heart by seeing her with another woman. I could scarcely believe this was even real. Never in a million years would I have imagined that Mackenzie would do this to me. After everything.

But I had seen for myself. Now I would have to go home and lick my wounds. Somehow I would go on without her. If that is what she wanted. And it was apparently what she wanted. I had never pictured her with anyone except me. On the short drive home, that is all I could see in my mind's eye. And to think that the bitch was even hitting on me right in front of Mackenzie. But then again she couldn't see. And I knew the sort of woman Kelly had been. The sort who had used her. And had never even given her flowers. Not once. How could she want her? I felt as if my heart would simply lose the will to beat. I went in my house, closed the door, and sat down on the floor in the dark to cry in private.

TWENTY-TWO: Betrayal

The phone startled me and I almost answered it. It had to be Mackenzie. Traitor. What could she possibly have to say to me, now? Sorry about your luck…I missed the selfish bull dyke. I was torn between heartbreak and rage. After all we had been through. And to do it this way. How could she? And I thought I knew her.

Now there was knocking on my door. "Sandy, lemme in." Becca called out from outside.

I crawled to my feet and opened the door without saying a word. I couldn't. It hurt to think much less speak. Becca held me close as only a good friend can. She did her best to comfort me. She patted me on the back and said, "There, there." She handed me a tissue. Even now she was giving me presents…a little pocket-sized packet of tissues. It made me laugh.

"Honey, you got the wrong impression over there." Becca announced. "Mackenzie asked me to come over and explain."

I cut her off by saying, "I could see what was going on…they just got out of the shower." Tears overwhelmed me as I said the words out loud. "My Mackenzie was with HER." I conceded.

"Sandy…that's not what happened." Becca said as she took my arm and pulled me down on the couch. With her free hand she turned on the lamp that was on the end table beside us.

"Oh yeah, well what did happen, then?" I asked.

"What happened is that Kelly heard about Mackenzie's accident and drove up from Florida…they are still friends, you know."

"Yeah, I saw…I'm not the blind one, remember." I chuffed and pouted feeling ever so wounded and shamelessly expressing it to Becca. I had nothing to hide from her. And she knew what Mackenzie and I had. Or what I thought we had. How could I have been so wrong about her?

"They had both showered…but not together, honey." Becca explained. "Mackenzie even locked the bathroom door while

133

she showered, ALONE..... do you hear me?" She said
as she grasped my shoulders and looked me in the eye. "You
jumped to conclusions."

"I know what I saw." I said, unwilling to roll over even though
all the wind was gone from my sails along with all the hope
from my heart. Hope for 'us'.

"Kelly does want to get back together…." Becca added.

"Well she can have her!" I shouted. "Tell her I said that…. if I
don't mean anything to Mackenzie, she can have that Kelly
person back."

"Now, I know you. And I know you aren't going to give up
without a fight." Becca stood to follow me. "I won't let you."

"Oh right, and I suppose I should go over there and kick
Kelly's…." I said sounding ridiculous even to myself. "Have
you seen that 'woman'…. she would throttle me." Both of us
knew I wouldn't enter into a fistfight. Not my style. Plus
Mackenzie had pushed me away.

"Mackenzie is having a hard time here…. and you have to fight
for her…stick with her." Becca started with a pep talk. "You
can't just give up and that…. that…. Kelly take her away."
Becca's words made me think. "I knew her with Kelly…and I
know her with you…. she belongs with YOU!"

"I won't do this, Becca." I said. "I appreciate what you are
trying to do here…but I won't do this."

"So you're just gonna give up?" Becca asked in disbelief.

"I'm gonna go to bed…and I'm gonna cry…and I'm going to
try to forget." I said. I choked on the word 'forget' because I
knew that it wasn't possible to forget Mackenzie Coleman.
But I would have to try. Heartbreak was like nothing I'd ever
known. And it seemed to swell in my chest with every breath
that filled my lungs.

Becca hugged me at the door. But there was no consoling me.
She had done her best. Maybe I should go over there and fight
for Mackenzie. I thought about it. Planned what I would say.
But that wasn't me. I didn't do that sort of drama. If

Mackenzie could turn her back on me and on the life we had built, I planned to let her do it. My heart would break right down the middle. But I had to let her be. All my life I had pushed. This, I could not…. would not push.

I kept to myself after that. For a long while I went nowhere. I was afraid I would see the two of them together. At the grocery or at the feed store. It would kill me, so I stayed at home. I guess I hid. Then, in spite of my hiding, I did see them. Over at Becca's in that intruder's truck. She helped Mackenzie out of the truck and into Becca's house. And she'd pushed me away because she thought I treated her like she was a 'helpless baby.' This was the worst emotion I'd ever felt. So I went inside. I closed the curtains and I tried not to imagine what I wondered they were doing over there. I longed to touch her face. Mackenzie's face. And run my fingers through her new hair. It looked longer and I felt so left out. I belonged with her. But I was alone.

I canned everything in sight. And I made Christmas presents. Candles and soap and jars of fig preserves. And then I plowed. Turning the soil with the tractor did my soul good. I could rev up the engine and turn tight circles. I made a big mess with the dirt. Then I fixed it perfectly. I thought ahead to the next crop I would plant. When I went back in the house I counted all the jars in my cellar and was proud of my accomplishments.

My phone rang one night and it was Barb, my childhood friend. I had been on her mind and she wondered if I needed something. When I told her what had happened she was dumbfounded. First that I had gotten romantically involved with a woman. And second that she'd dumped me…. just like that. Then she expressed pride at how far I had come…. the horses, the crops, the canned goods, and all. But she'd always known I would succeed at whatever I tried to do. Talking with her bolstered my spirits. She had asked if there was anyone else. "No…except for my vet, but he's too pushy and my heart hurts." I admitted. She understood and wished me well. We planned for her to visit as soon as she was free. It was good to hear all about her husband and her kids. Happy little life…. but it belonged to someone else.

Fishing gave me time to think. And it gave me more
things to squirrel away in my freezer. As I cleaned a fish one
day, a bream I think (southern for bluegill) I thought back to
fishing on that very pond with my granddaddy. Once he'd
accidentally hooked me in the head with a lure that had three
sets of hooks. All three hooks had ended up in the back of my
head. I had cried. Not because it hurt but because we had to
leave the pond and drive into town to find the doctor. He'd
shaved part of my hair off.... around the fishhook. Just like
Mackenzie's hair. Except they had shaved her entire head. I
enjoyed fishing, but even that made me miss Mackenzie and
think of her. The bobber bounced up and down in the water.
And my thoughts bounced down the road to her.

Life had a way of going on. My mother called and we chatted.
She could tell I was sad, but I didn't say why. Becca kept me
company as much as she could with a family of her own to
spoil. I was doing okay though and even though I was sad
about Mackenzie, I didn't miss my old life at all. Not one bit.
The corporate world was my relic. Now I was a farmer and an
Arabian horse breeder. As I sat on my porch surveying things
and taking inventory on my life, it hit me. I needed a barn.
With babies on the way I needed stalls. Even though I ascribed
to the unconventional viewpoint that mares should foal outside,
I at least needed the option of stalls. In case of bad weather or
injuries...or potential buyers. When people shop for horses,
they expect to see barns. My horses were content being out in
the elements. But as I sat taking stock, I decided it was time
for action.

I went online and did more research. I learned everything I
could about barns and the various companies in North Georgia
who build them. Prices varied, but I still had a substantial nest
egg at my fingertips. Becca offered suggestions over lunch.
And we walked around with a little measuring wheel she'd
brought over to help us choose the spot. When she brought up
the idea of a concrete pad for a shoeing area, my heartache
awoke anew. We talked about the inevitable...who we would
use to care for our horses now that Mackenzie was out of the
picture. She gave me a business card and told me the guy was

"so-so." I knew she wanted to say he wasn't as good as Mackenzie, but she didn't want to twist the knife that was still lodged in that wound. When I asked if she'd talked with Mackenzie, she said that she had not. Mackenzie had turned into something of a hermit after Kelly left.

"Kelly left?" I asked. "When?" I didn't even attempt to hide my relief from Becca because she knew me. And she knew I would never stop wanting Mackenzie back.

"A couple of weeks ago…she went back to Florida where she lives." Becca informed me what little she knew.

"And you know this how?" I probed further.

"Mackenzie told me…but that's all she would say." Becca elaborated. "And she made it clear she didn't want to talk about any of it…especially you." She had called our mutual friend to ask for help with grocery shopping. Mackenzie would write out a list for her once a week and Becca would do her shopping. She didn't eat much. Neither had I over the last few months. Heartbreak does that to some people.

As I looked over pictures of the barn I'd chosen, I wondered what Mackenzie would think of it. It was strange reorienting my life without her. It was also strange that she had not called me. Not once. Not even after that woman, using the term loosely, had left for Florida. Should I call her? That question haunted me day and night. The lock of her hair in my alabaster keepsake box still smelled like her. That musky rain woman smell I adored. But she was nowhere else in my life right now. And I felt her slipping away with the passage of each day of my life.

The builders arrived on a Monday morning. And the foreman seemed impressed with all my ideas and my measurements. We discussed the placement of windows and things based on the position of the sun during different times of the day. He wanted to know why I wanted the barn isle so wide. When I told him I had a 'close friend' who was a horseshoer and that she'd commented that barn isles should be big, he asked, "Mackenzie?" It didn't really surprise me since most people here knew her. She was also the only female farrier in our area. "How is she...after what happened?" He asked.

"It's been quite an adjustment..." I said fighting back the tears that clawed their way to the surface. I turned away and focused my attention on the details of the barn. They broke ground that afternoon. Then they poured the foundation. It would take about two months to complete the project. I took pictures each night as my barn began to take shape. It really was a beautiful structure, and my granddaddy would approve if he could see. So would Mackenzie.

Anything made out of wood has character, I think. As I sat on the porch watching the progress near the end, I thought about how much I like the smell of wood. It smells like emerging life. Appropriate for this incubator of sorts. Meant to shelter new horse life. While my barn was being built, I read. All about birthing horses. I learned about 'imprinting' and decided to try it when my youngsters arrived. This belief was that if you exposed a newborn foal to all sorts of stimuli, you could desensitize it to many of the things that would otherwise frighten it later. Since horses have to learn fast in the wild, they are like little sponges when they hit the ground. If you can de-spook them within the first twenty-four hours of their lives they will be bombproof later. That theory made sense to my analytical brain. And I didn't buy into that 'crazy Arab' theory that many people have about horses. My girls had always been calm...as calm as a hot-blooded horse can be, I suppose.

I made my imprinting list one day on the porch. Water, garden hoses, the feel of concrete underfoot, tractor noise, dog's barking, plastic bags, hats, being touched all over, and picking up your feet, the sound of trimming tools. All things seemed to lead right back to Mackenzie. The horseshoe she'd given me was still on the porch beside me. I decided to nail it over the barn door, just under the hayloft. After they had delivered and stacked my hay, I climbed the stairs to the loft. As I sat down on the sweet-smelling bale of hay, I started to cry. Again. Because I remembered Mackenzie's hayloft that night. No hay. Our nest. I missed her and wondered if she would ever see again. And I wondered what she would think of my barn and my hayloft. I also wondered if she had all those memories imprinted so deeply in her heart like I did. Imprinted...just like a baby horse.

Becca and Tim arrived one morning as I was hammering the horseshoe on my new barn. They brought a barn-warming present. Clad in overalls, Tim pushed the new wheelbarrow and looked the part. Inside were goodies. A green plastic pitchfork, a coiled garden hose, a leaf rake, and a scoop shovel. All very practical. They had always had a knack for choosing gifts that were perfect. And it always left me feeling grateful yet undeserving. I admired their giving nature. They seemed to have so much fun doing things for other people.

"Coffee?" I asked as I pointed towards the house.

"Twist my arm." Tim offered with his teddy-bear smile. The teddy bear and the cherub sat on the porch and drank coffee with me. We admired the barn pointing out all of its good design, placement, and features. The workers really had done a good job. Money well spent.

"Let's introduce the horses." Tim said as he stood and reached for my hand.

"No time like the present." I agreed. "I could use your help, actually." It was good that there were three of us. Change is not a welcome thing for horses. Probably because they are creatures of prey. I had read that any kind of change can signal doom for a horse in the wild. So they memorize their immediate environment. When something is out of place, it might mean disaster. Like a blind person, they feel secure when things are all in their proper places. Something new might mean a mountain lion and the end of their life. So they ran...just like Mackenzie had done.

Even though they had watched the barn being built, they were wary about going in. Some people think horses are stupid creatures. Just because they think like prey animals. It would be stupid to not be cautious about this. But that is just another reflection of the arrogance of human beings. We talked about all that and we slowly coaxed them into the virgin barn. They

139

trusted us. And we took our time. But we didn't close them in the stalls. We opened the gate at the back of each stall's turnout. That allowed them into the arena. The gate at the far end of the arena allowed them access to the rest of the property including the pond. It was a series of gates that all led to more freedom. They were free to choose. Security and shelter, grass and water, and trees and fresh air. Sunshine or rain. I left it up to them. Just as I left it up to my cats. They had a little doggy door, but they spent most of the time outside.

I had also left it all up to Mackenzie. It seemed as if she'd chosen freedom as well. Or seclusion, or isolation, or whatever it was. All I knew was that she wasn't there. She was no longer a part of the passing days of my life. Or of the long nights that I entertained myself by reading. Without flickering candlelight.

TWENTY-THREE: Decisions

Even though I lived out in the country and in a low crime area I began to feel uneasy living alone. Television, though I watched seldom, did little to quell those fears. The weekly newspaper included reports of crimes in the area. It seems our village wasn't immune to or untouched by crime. Women were raped, houses were burglarized, and property was stolen. At night, before bed, I started checking the windows and doors to make sure they were locked. I slept with a hammer beside my bed...my hi-tech security system. When living in the city, I had read once that the police were looking for a man who had sustained severe injuries to the nose and face that were made by the claw end of a hammer. He had evidently tried to rape the wrong woman. I had bought myself a hammer that day. A big one. Not one of those wimpy-girly-household-tool-box-kind-of hammers most women own. Mine was a twenty-four ounce Vaughn framing hammer. It looked like you could split wood with the thing. Or an attacker's face. It gave me goose bumps to think about these things.

I also didn't own a dog. Never had. I liked dogs, but I just preferred cats as household pets. I'd read about cats that protected the Pharaohs of ancient Egypt. My cats were about as protective as a goldfish. Adopting a dog...a farm dog for outside might be a good idea. It was a thought that I gave more serious consideration when things started getting moved. I would leave a book in the barn and find it later on the porch. Odd. Or, the hose I had painstakingly coiled would be strewn out in disarray. Even odder. Why would a robber water flowers or read a book while he was there? I wondered if I were suffering from memory loss. So I purposely left things out and wrote down when and where. I even left out money once... a five-dollar bill. The next morning it was gone. Or for a while I thought it was gone. I found it folded and under the brick doorstop on my porch. I had left it crumpled yet out in the open tucked into the base of a flowerpot. So someone had found it and instead of stealing it, he'd pressed out all the wrinkles, folded it in half, and tucked it under the brick.

Someone who was toying with me. Trying to frighten
me. It was working.

When I discussed all this with Becca she said she'd keep an
eye on things. A closer eye. Not long after that she was riding
her horse in my round pen when I got home from the grocery.

"Hey, Goldilocks" I said to her playfully even though her hair
wasn't blonde. "So you like my round pen better than yours, I
see."

"Not why I'm here." She said in a serious tone as she
dismounted and led the horse towards me. "Saw somebody on
your porch." She reported. Breath froze in my lungs. "But
when I got here he was gone. Tim looked around before he left
for work, but I thought you should know before you went in."
She added. "I'll go in with you." She tied her horse to the
hitching rail and held my hand.

Nothing was disturbed…no forced entry. But the rocking
chairs had been moved. Two were facing each other as if he'd
sat there with his feet propped up. In my rocking chair on my
porch. I felt violated and angry. Even though we searched
around and found everything else as it should be. I decided
then and there to get a dog. A big protective dog…like a
German shepherd. There was a dog shelter in the county, and
Becca agreed to go with me the next day to pick out a dog. I
knew my cats wouldn't like the idea. And I hoped that the dog
I'd get would be protective yet gentle with my cats.

The next morning I woke up thinking about dog names.
Naming a pet is a serious responsibility. I had on flannel
pajamas and a terry-cloth bathrobe. Coffee would help me
think. And I would make a list. That is how I had always
functioned in the business world. So I sat down at my kitchen
table as the emerging sun was shedding light on my list. Since
I wasn't sure whether I would choose a boy or a girl dog, I had
listed both. I refilled my cup of coffee and tucked the list into
my pocket. Thinking would be better out in the fresh air of the
porch. I unlocked the deadbolt and slipped on my shoes. One
of the horses whinnied a greeting. I thought of another name
for my list. When I reached in my pocket for the paper list, I

pulled out the wine cork instead. From that first night home from the hospital with Mackenzie. Tears filled my eyes as I was caught off guard by the recollection. With my mind miles away on the past I barely noticed the movement. Barely heard the rocking chair move. But I heard it. Someone was sitting in the rocking chair!"

I tried to scream, but no sound escaped me. Just as I lunged for the safety of the open door, she spoke. Mackenzie. I froze in my tracks, no longer afraid but confused.

"Hey…sorry to frighten you." She said as she continued to rock.

I wanted to run to her and grab her in my arms. Or slap her. I wanted to kiss her with all the pent-up passion inside of me. Or yell at her for scaring me. For pushing me away in the first place. For being almost naked alone in the house with her ex. For letting her help her in from the truck at Becca's. I wanted to rush to her and beg her to stay. But my voice was still not working at all. So I was grateful when she spoke again even though she seemed so serious.

"I've been coming here a lot." She said with almost no emotion in her voice. She wasn't even looking towards me as she spoke. But she was blind and adjusting to that reality. "Good place to think." She said as she swept an arm upward displaying my porch.

"That was you?" I asked realizing that Mackenzie had been the one. "Why didn't you? …" But then I knew. She had not wanted to talk…to confront me. Until today. She had not attempted to scurry off when I opened the door. She had not even stopped rocking in the chair. I was so glad to finally see her face to face that I couldn't say even one word about my fears of an attacker. Or my decision to adopt a guard dog. But I wasn't sure what I would do. What I should do.

"Can a woman get a cup of coffee around here?" She asked, still facing away and speaking deliberately and with little inflection in her voice.

"Sure." I agreed. As I poured the coffee into her special mug I remembered all the times we had shared coffee on the porch together. This time felt awkward. I searched my mind and my vocabulary for what to say. How to say it. I couldn't tell what was going on here. I wasn't awake. And I wasn't sure why she was even here. I assumed the worst. She was moving away....going to Florida to be with Kelly. She must be here to break the news. My hand holding the cup was shaking. So was my feeble heart. At least she wasn't gone yet. But I knew her. Once she decided something, she didn't change her mind. Should I try to change it...her mind? Or should I just let her go? She was already gone from my life. My bed. But she was on my porch. I put the cups on the tray and blew my nose in a paper towel.

When I opened the door, there she was. I had not heard her move. Had she fallen? She was kneeling just in front of me as I stepped through the door. I put down the tray with the cups. As I reached to help her she lifted up her head, held out one hand, and spoke. There was something in her hand. She was offering it to me.

"Sandy," she spoke through tears, "Will you marry me?" The thing she was stretching out to offer me was a ring. Was I dreaming? Was she saying what I thought she was saying? What I had wanted to say to her? What I had lived to hear, to think, to plan?

When I reached, or more appropriately dove for the ring, I dislodged it from her outstretched hand. We fumbled for it. I guess since I could see it in the early-morning light, I touched it first. And then I kissed her. She kissed back with a newfound tenderness. And tears. Our faces were awash with them. I checked to make sure the ring wasn't loose on my finger as I encompassed her kneeling frame. We cried and we held each other tightly. And we kissed some more.

"Well?" When she asked again I realized I had not answered.

"Yes, Mackenzie, I would be honored to marry you!" I laughed and sang all at the same time. Never before had I been so overcome, so surprised and so happy. All in an instant. Just

144

like that instant that had changed things forever. But this was far happier. Jubilant. Triumphant.

"So, does that mean you forgive me, too?" Mackenzie asked as she slid to a sitting position in front of me. "Cause I was an ass...and I'm truly sorry." Tears lent credibility to her apology.

I brushed her tears away and held her face before me. "Of course, I forgive you, honey....will you forgive me, too?" I begged.

"I did that already." She said. "And I hated myself for pushing you away. But I had to...I had to see if I could do it alone.... I had to know I could..." Now she was brushing my tears away. She was so strong. To face blindness all alone. To push away the one person who would take over and do everything for her willingly.

"I missed you so much." I said. "Lemme hold you for a long time." Right there on my porch where it all started, we kissed again. We held each other, I looked carefully into her pretty face, ran my fingers through her hair that had grown back, and kissed familiar lips. She traced my face, studying all the lines and contours.

"I missed you more than I could begin to say." She relayed. "I'm sorry I was mean...you know I adore you...love what we have."

"Enough." I proclaimed. "Our coffee's getting cold."

So we sat on the porch, in the same rocking chair like we had done many times, and drank all the coffee that I had made. She told me she was afraid. Afraid to have lost her eyesight. Afraid of all that blindness had changed. And she was afraid of not being able to work ever again...to earn a living shoeing horses. Afraid of losing her house. Mostly afraid of losing me.

She was afraid I would get tired of being with a blind person. She was afraid I would want her out of my life. Afraid she would be a burden.

How could I turn myself inside and out? How could I convince her that I could never feel that way about her? "Mackenzie, I could never feel that way about you!" I declared. "You are the reason my heart beats." I promised. "I don't care if you're blind, or broke, or anything else….just as long as you want me." She knew. If not, she wouldn't have spent all that time thinking and wound up on my porch proposing marriage. And I had wholeheartedly and convincingly accepted. We gradually started to smile and the flood of tears subsided. We sat on my porch and made all the decisions…together.

First, we decided when and where to get married. It would be outside in my yard…in early April. Our families and friends would be invited and we would ride off on horseback together. That was something Mackenzie had not done since her accident, but we had time to prepare. We decided that we would even go to the beach for a few days for a honeymoon…to Jekyll Island. I had not been there since I was a teenager, and I felt much like a teenager in love all over again. Even though the state of Georgia wouldn't recognize our marriage, it was important to us to make it official. For us. And for our families. As I thought about the disarray of the institution of marriage among heterosexuals, I wondered why they are so threatened by what we share. But we were not ready to take on social causes. We cared only about each other and proclaiming our love to the world. I had accepted Mackenzie's proposal without a moment's hesitation even though I had vowed never to marry again after my ugly divorce. I wanted nothing more than this. We had found what most people long all their lives to find. Many straight people had a marriage license that didn't mean a thing. We had so much more.

"So is this married couple going to live together?" She asked, broaching the subject of our future living arrangements.

"Let's." I replied succinctly. "My place or yours?" I asked and realized that I was sounding like someone with a pickup line instead of a woman in her forties planning marriage.

"I won't ask you to sell your place." Mackenzie became serious as she spoke. "This land, this cabin has been in your family for generations. My place has no sentimental value…except for what we added."

"So you wanna move in with me, then?" I asked, elated at the thought of having her right here with me all the time. "As long as you're okay with selling your house and all."

"You do realize I come with animals….seven horses…and Mitch?" She reminded me of what I had already anticipated. Mitch was no trouble at all. And I wouldn't need to adopt a dog. He got along fine with my cats since he had long since acquired a healthy respect for their claws. And there was plenty of room for the horses. My farm was growing. But it still didn't yet have a name. Not for long. We tossed around ideas and settled on "Plan B Farm". Sometimes life takes a course different than the one we had planned. So we go with 'Plan B'. Catchy name. I thought of where we could hang the sign once we had one made.

As we drank coffee and discussed the details of all our decisions, I found myself feeling for my new ring. Mackenzie had ordered it from a catalog with Becca's help. On it was inscribed "Por Tous Jour", which is French and means "For Always." Life has its share of surprises. And not all of them are unwelcome. This day was proving that to be true.

We talked about all that awful time apart. She had bruises on her shins from learning where all her furniture was positioned. And her horses had not cooperated when it came time for feeding. I told how I'd kept busy during her absence. She admired the barn after being led throughout. Then she told me all about Kelly. Mackenzie had actually considered getting back together with that rough woman. Only because it would be easy. Easy to depend on someone she didn't love. Someone she did not respect. It would be a bond of convenience. But she couldn't bring herself to hurt me that way or to leave the state. That would have finalized our parting. Plus, even though she was blind, she could see that I still had left open a place for her in my life. She could feel it when she sat on my porch. And she couldn't picture herself

anywhere else. As she began to wrap her mind around
the fact that she was blind, she had come to the realization that
it really didn't matter to me. She knew I would make whatever
adjustments her blindness presented. Because she knew in her
soul that we were meant to be together. That I loved her as no
one ever had or would. Our souls had touched. She had felt
that, too.

"Wanna see the hayloft?" I asked, forgetting that she was
blind. "I'm sorry…" I started to apologize.

"Don't do that." She said. "It really is okay to use the word
'see' around me." She really had come to terms with all this.
Her voice showed that. "And yes, I would love to see your
hayloft." She finished as she dropped her cane and reached for
my arm. While we were making our way up the stairs I
formulated a plan. I showed her around and then I whispered
softly in her ear, "Sit down right here, Honey," as I patted a
bale of hay away from the window. Then I gently unbuttoned
her blouse and draped it behind her and kissed her neck on its
way down to the hay.

"The hayloft is the best part of a barn, don't you think?" I
asked. It made me happy to flirt with her anew.

She said nothing. Reaching up, she grabbed the back of my
head and pulled me down to where she was. And she felt her
way into my flannel pajamas. They were getting hot anyway.
The bathrobe became another blanket-of-sorts on the hay. We
certainly had not forgotten each other. My hayloft…our
hayloft had been properly christened.

Her whistle startled us both. Becca was on horseback in my
front yard. She was calling out towards the open screen door.
But we were in the barn. In the hayloft. We grabbed for
strewn clothes. Fortunately we were nowhere near the
window.

"Up here." I called to her through the loft's window as I tied
the tie on my bathrobe. "Be right down." I added as I helped
Mackenzie into her jeans. She had already buttoned up her
shirt. Pajamas in hand, I made my way down the stairs.

Mackenzie held my arm. Touched my bum. She had such a way.

"Oh good….you're here." Becca said when she saw Mackenzie had been with me in the loft. Then she realized Mackenzie had been with me in the loft, literally. Instead of being offended, I thought she would jump for joy. She leapt from the horse. Kissed me on the cheek and whispered, "I told you…" Never had I been so glad to have been wrong. When she saw the pajamas she grinned. She also noticed Mackenzie's shirt was buttoned up all wrong. "Sorry if I interrupted…" She started to say.

"We need your help…planning a wedding." Mackenzie smiled a contented smile as she spoke. "Sandy said 'Yes'!" I remembered Becca had helped her order the ring. A deep sigh escaped me.

"I would love nothing better." Becca said. "You know I love you both." She reminded us. When she kissed us each on the cheek I wondered if she noticed anything. We had been busy in the hayloft. Re-uniting. Sealing our engagement.

Becca visited for a little while. Then she pretended she had something to do. And her horse needed to go. Her excuses had been for our benefit. "I can't wait to tell Tim." She smiled and waved as she rode away at a trot. Her horse even seemed excited.

We went in and took a shower together. A long loving shower. Afterwards I made breakfast. Even though it was afternoon, we wanted breakfast. Then we found the number for a realtor. Mackenzie made the phone call. But we would be together for the appointment…the appraisal. Her house was going on the market. We decided to move the horses right away. And Mitch. Her truck and trailer would make the job easy. So we dressed in work clothes. Jeans, t-shirts and gloves for handling the lead ropes. Her horses all loaded easily. Maybe they thought we were going on a trip. Mackenzie had planned who would go in first and the like. Hauling horses can be tricky. If you put the wrong two next to each other, the trip can be ugly. She kept her distance and listened as I loaded each one.

Instructions about who to tie short, who to give slack reminded me how well she understood horses. It was going to be good to have her at Plan B Farm. And I was glad that my life had not gone according to plan. Except that all along I had planned on being happy somehow. I never anticipated being this happy, though. Not remotely.

TWENTY-FOUR: Road Trip

It seemed to take no time at all to sell Mackenzie's house. After we had moved her horses to 'our' house, we spruced her place up somewhat. Not long after that we handed over the key to the new owners. And I wondered about the young couple that had bought my house long ago in Ohio. That seemed like another life. It certainly had been quite another life.

Mackenzie sold some of her belongings in a yard sale, but most of her furniture was now in my house. We had plenty of room. We had to cautiously arrange everything though since Mackenzie couldn't see. I was careful not to move things like the ottoman since they might trip her as she moved through our home. It didn't take long to refer to my cabin as 'our house' and things seemed as if our lives fit well together. Other people thought so, as well. We got a fair price for her house. And she wanted to use the money to invest in a new career for herself. So she wouldn't be a burden to me. Several careers came to mind, but they held no interest for her.

Slowly, gloom settled over her like unwanted storm clouds. Or the rust on her anvil. When I mentioned a possible new career one day Mackenzie fumed aloud, "I never wanted a new career!" All she had done for a living was shoe horses. It had to be difficult for her to no longer work at what she loved. I had to help her through this. We had met with the counselor the doctor in Atlanta had recommended. Communication is an art and we were learning the rudimentary skills.

"I'm sure that's true, Honey." I said being careful not to call her 'Baby' in this precarious context. "But we'll think of something you might like doing…. there's no hurry." I added. I was glad that we were not in a position where we had to fret about financial matters.

The realization that Mackenzie could no longer perform the work she loved had hit her harder than the hoof that had blinded her. Muscles that were once taut on her body were softening, but she was still fit looking. I could tell she missed not just the work but also the horses that belonged to her clients. So I suggested we go visit a few of them. The people agreed and said that they had missed her regular visits. Each time we visited a client, she would greet the horse. Then she would lay down her cane and reach out for the horse. Each horse seemed to sense her blindness and stood cautiously under her caress. She whispered softly to them and they relaxed. Not once though did she attempt to pick up any horse's foot. That was over for her. Her hands were strong but they would no longer do the work of caring for hooves. She had caressed her tools like they were precious memories in a keepsake box. But she could no longer operate them. That fact made us all sad. It made her clients sad as well. But it was a reality we were all accepting.

Then one day she asked to go see Dusty. Dusty was the horse that had kicked her. She had been thinking about it a great deal. Ever since she had been told which horse kicked her, she had known this day would arrive. Mackenzie wasn't the type of person to shrink from fear. After all, she'd pushed me away and forced herself to make it on her own…blind. And she had succeeded. Now she wanted to face the same horse that had plunged her into darkness and changed life forever in the process. The owners seemed hesitant. Since their horse had hurt her so badly they were afraid something even worse would happen. They felt guilty already even though Mackenzie had graciously assured them that she blamed neither them nor their horse. She'd been told that a dog had startled the horse resulting in the kick that had been intended for the dog. But Mackenzie didn't even blame the dog.

"That's why they call these things accidents." Mackenzie laughed as she spoke. "And Dusty probably wonders where I am." She said thoughtfully. So the people agreed for us to visit.

When we arrived the owner held the horse. As I had done with the others, I let Mackenzie take my arm as we approached the horse. Dusty lowered his big old head and gently pushed it under Mackenzie's left arm. She said, "Hey, big fella…how've you been?" That horse seemed to know. And it was apparent by the way Mackenzie stroked him that she'd forgiven him for hurting her. She rubbed his face and stroked his muscular neck. When she reached a spot along his spine, he flinched.

"His back has been sore since our last ride the other day." The owner said. "But he seems to like that." We watched as Mackenzie massaged his back. The horse melted and relaxed under her touch. I knew the feeling. Her hands found tension then released it like a dove. At that instant I knew. Mackenzie would become an equine massage therapist. Her hands held the necessary strength. She had a way with horses. They softened under her touch. And she didn't need to see in order to massage them. I was glad the owner said it. "You'd be a good massage therapist, Mac…something to think about." Not much was said for the rest of our visit. But I knew Mackenzie was pondering over the suggestion.

All the way home, Mackenzie was silent. Then she said softly as she smelled her hands, "It's good to smell like a horse again." We were both glad that she'd been visiting the horses. And we discussed how good it had felt to overcome her fear. It was justified but it stood in her way like a piece of furniture that had been moved into the wrong place. Progress was a constant for Mackenzie even though she could no longer see. Her hair wasn't the only thing growing. Not wanting to push, I waited. And then later that afternoon, she asked the question that kept surfacing in our minds. "Do you think I could learn to be a massage therapist…for horses?" She asked tentatively.

"Of course you could." I reached for her hand and smiled. "You are good with your hands." I said sincerely and flirtatiously.

"Will you help me?" She asked as she began to smile at the idea of a new career.

"Sure…wanna practice on me?" I asked with a whinny laugh.

"No, I'm serious, Sandy." She said with a frown forming in her brow. "Will you help me find a school? One that will take me even though I'm blind." As she spoke she massaged my

hand as she considered a new trade. Horses though.
And that was a good thing. She was good with them, and they
responded well to her touch.

"Absolutely." I agreed. "I'll start right now." My computer
buzzed as I searched Google for 'Equine Massage Therapy'
information. I found out about books and schools and
excitedly read her the information. Finding the books in
Braille was going to be difficult. But I had agreed to help.
That included reading aloud to her. And she could learn the
muscle groups with help…or on our horses. Her spirit seemed
to be reviving itself as she spoke about it all. Like a stiff
muscle, her soul seemed to creak yet give way to hope. It felt
so sweet.

"After practice, let's go out and celebrate…" She said
playfully. "Can I still practice on you?" She asked as she
simultaneously kissed my neck and began to massage my
shoulders.

"Lower." I sighed.

"Here?" She asked as she pulled me towards the unmade bed.

"Lower." I moaned this time as she both massaged and
caressed me.

"Your clothes are getting in the way." She whined. And then
she did something I adored in a lover. She picked me up,
slammed me onto the bed, and tore off my clothes. It made my
heart race. A woman on a mission. And a woman with a
renewed sense of passion. Not just for me but for life, as well.

Afterwards, while she was running the water for our bath, I
made our reservations. At Pasquali's. The romantic Italian
restaurant had been the place we went on our first date. I
thought about the necklace, and the tulips. And I joined her in
the bubbles of the bathtub. She had even lit candles. She
might be blind, but her romantic nature had not dimmed.
Neither had mine. Nor had my hope for our future. Through
the water and amid the bubbles she began to practice
massaging. I was so happy about her new career choice.

During dinner we laughed. We made all kinds of plans. She asked me if I would help her call all her customers to tell them her idea. She needed me to at least look up the names and read the phone numbers to her from her customer book. I was glad to have the time to help her with all of this. My new life afforded me a great many things worthwhile. As our spirits soared in celebration, we decided to go on a trip. The quaint town of Helen, Georgia wasn't that far away. And we needed an outing. Becca and Tim would agree to watch our menagerie. We had never been on a trip together. This was going to be fun.

During the short drive to the village of Helen, we stopped only once. On the side of the road I had seen a shrine of sorts. It was a giant cast iron pot with steaming peanuts bobbing up and down like synchronized swimmers. The crusty fella who stirred the pot dipped them out of the hot salty water with a huge ladle. Filling the plastic-lined brown paper bags, he moved carefully. We bought four of the biggest bags and sped on our way eating as we went. The warm juice and the succulent peanuts tasted divine. Out the window went the peanut hulls like the bad mood we had shed. When we pulled into the parking lot and looked around it seemed like we had driven all the way to Switzerland. All the building edifices had been transformed years ago to resemble an alpine village. Street names had been changed, as well. Tourists now flocked to this remote mountain town. It had been a marketing coup for the people here. We dined on all sorts of European food and strolled the few blocks of the town arm in arm. Being blind had its advantages.

Mackenzie and I had never been more in love with each other. Or with each other's bodies. One night in the flickering candlelight of our pseudo-Swiss motel room, I tried something daring. I had experimented on myself at home alone, so I knew it wouldn't hurt her. I told her what to expect…hot candle wax. She was on her back on our bed with the covers down around her feet. Her nipples stood at attention. Waiting for what I'd explained…what I was going to do. As I tipped the pine candle on its side, the hot wax dripped onto her attentive nipple. She moaned and my mouth watered.

"You like that?" I asked. Watching her body react had already told me that she did. So I dribbled more wax on her other nipple. Brown pebbles on olive skin. Pine- green candle wax blanketed her and froze in place. Her body was a masterpiece in that bed. I put the candle on the bedside table so I could move. As skill follows familiarity, we had learned how to please each other. She could make me wet with just a sigh. No matter how frustrated she had been about her unwanted blindness, she never was awkward or uncertain in bed. Especially not now that the world was out there. On the other side of a locked door in a town where nobody knew us or cared who we were. Or that we were two women who were madly in love with each other.

One night, I decided we should shower and dress and get some fresh air. So I phoned a carriage service and made an appointment. Riding was something we had both missed. We would ride again soon. It was in our plans for the days ahead. But for now this was a safe and romantic alternative. Sitting close under the lap blanket, we made out in the night air. The clop of the horse's hooves on the pavement kept tempo with my heartbeats. And hers. She noticed that the driving horse was a little off on one of his hooves…her trained ear could hear it.

"I used to be a farrier." She told the carriage driver.

"Hard to find a good one." The driver said referring to a good farrier or horseshoer.

"When you do, you gotta keep em happy." I agreed but I wasn't referring to anything professional. Proving that, my hands wandered underneath the blanket. And I kissed Mackenzie deeply thrusting my tongue into her soft mouth.

When she looked at me, I could swear she could still see me. At least she'd been able to see the look in my eyes the first time I'd boldly professed my love for her out loud. And she could remember. We could both remember all that had transpired to link us together emotionally. I also knew that a

156

local florist was delivering flowers to our room. Tulips. For later.

During what remained of our trip to Helen, we discussed more of the details of our wedding. We agreed on most things, which made it easier. Unlike my first marriage. I had hated my ex-husbands tastes in font styles, china patterns, and even shoes. But in the long run, he didn't even like me, so this time around had to be better. It was almost time to send out the invitations, and Becca and I had already addressed them all. Most of our family members had agreed to take part or to at least attend the ceremony. The most prominent holdout was Mackenzie's brother. He thought he was better than everybody else including Mackenzie now that she was a big shot lawyer. He also had voiced her disapproval of her lowly farrier sister's 'lifestyle' even though he'd initially been cool about it when Mackenzie had come out to him in a letter. I wondered how anyone could ostracize his only sibling like that. It hurt Mackenzie deeply since she'd always tried to be a good sister and also because the lawyer was her only sibling. Mackenzie was only being herself. What other choice did she have? It always amazes me when intelligent people make such ignorant and narrow-minded choices. Especially when it hurts members of their own families. I thought blood was thicker than water. Not knowing Mackenzie and not being involved in the life of such a giving and interesting person had to be her brother's loss. At least that was my conclusion about the whole thing. I was however extremely biased.

With the wedding only a few weeks away, I began to look forward to all the festivities. And I longed for another romantic interlude with the woman I grew to adore with each new synapse. Our next trip would be our honeymoon at the beach. We had a great many things to do before we could welcome that day's arrival. I needed to make a new list.

TWENTY-FIVE: Riding Again

A few days after our trip to Helen, I decided it was time. Early one morning, I saddled up Scout and Princess Jazmine. They were both about the same size and I could pony Scout. Even though Mackenzie could no longer see, we were going to ride our horses. It was time. She didn't want to be viewed as a helpless person, and I was ready to oblige. Our morning rides were something that we both missed. It was, after all where we had fallen in love. Riding horses. After coffee on the porch I said, "Get your boots on, we're going riding."

"You're kidding…" she trailed off in a half question half exclamation.

"Ask the horses if I'm kidding." I declared boldly. "They're all dressed up and ready to go." I alerted her to the fact that I had saddled both horses. "It's all training, remember?" She smiled when I reminded of her of her own words months earlier when she'd provided me with the same surprise. Only this time it was training for her now that she had a disability.

"What the hell," she said after digesting the idea. "After all, I'm already hurt."

"That's the spirit." I chuckled as we walked. "Silver lining in every cloud." I hoped silently that Scout would eventually become a guide pony of sorts. He had the disposition for it.

"Guess I can't exactly use this." She said as she discarded her cane by the hitching rail. "Point me in the right direction, please."

"Right this way, Ma'am." I guided her towards the horse as I spoke.

"Hey Scout…good choice, Sandy." She had felt for recognition and approved of my choice of her mount.

"I know what you need." I reminded her with pride.

"No doubt about that fact." She agreed. "But will you pony me just in case?" When she took the reins in her hands I noticed that they were both shaking. Her breathing kept pace. She forced out a breath. Scout seemed to sense her nervousness and turned towards her with a protective nudge. He stood still as a post.

"You bet." I answered. "Not about to let you run off and leave me this close to the wedding." She pulled me close and kissed me longingly. Instead of breaking us, her accident had pulled us inexorably together like grafted trees. We were becoming one in the same. Neither of us wanted to sever that bond even though I would gladly live out my life in the dark if only Mackenzie could see. And shoe horses. And ride without my help. But sometimes in life, we must learn to accept our circumstances and make the best of things. Bitterness makes people old and ugly. Neither of us saw that as a solution.

I helped Mackenzie onto Scout and while she adjusted herself I walked around her horse and mounted my own. Both horses seemed to know. They were on their best behavior. It felt good to be in the sun and on the back of a horse again. We walked leisurely around in the spring grass. The woman of my dreams was tethered to me by a long lead line. But she instinctively reined Scout back when he started going too fast for her comfort. I wish I were as good a rider as she was even though she was now blind. I had always envied her balance. She looked so natural atop a horse. Moving freely seemed to agree with her.

"This is different." She said as her hands continued to tremble. "I don't know what I should do since I can't see what's ahead." She added. "Don't tell anybody, but I'm scared s----less." As she admitted it, the fear seemed to dissipate.

"I've got you." I said as I tightened my grip on Scout's lead line as a reminder to her and to the horse.

"I'm sure you do...but close your eyes long enough to realize how strange this feels and you'll see what I mean." She said sounding almost lost inside.

I could only do it for an instant because we were still moving. "You're right. It is scary. And you're the bravest person I know."

"Any phone booths around? I need to change
clothes." Mackenzie said with an ingratiating smile that spread
across her face.

"Not for miles." I told her what she already knew.

"Too bad." She mused out loud. "I guess I'll keep this
disguise on then."

We rode that day for almost an hour. At a lazy walk that we all
enjoyed. From then on, we rode every day. Several times
Becca joined us on our meandering rides. The horses seemed
to enjoy the lazy pace as much as we did. And even though
Scout seemed to know Mackenzie needed him to behave, I still
kept him on a long lead line. The thought of the horse going
out of control didn't set well with me. Neither of us could
afford another injury.

All we did need was the fresh air and the good feeling that
comes from being on the back of a horse in the sunshine. The
breezes seemed to inflate our souls. We continued our ritual.
Lovemaking at daybreak. Coffee on the porch. Long lazy
horse rides in the sunshine. Not always in that order.

Our lives seemed to center around horses. When we were not
busy with wedding plans, we were attending to our horses in
some fashion or another. They got long luxurious baths and
daily brushing. They were all shedding as horses do when
spring arrives. Wads of horsehair made the birds happy. It
was cute to look up in a tree and see a nest that was made out
of the hair of our horses. The symbiotic aspects of our farm
were far-reaching and everywhere. Even our animals
depended on each other for warmth and safety. And it
furthered the feelings of home and family that we were
building at the Ole Plan B Farm.

I eventually had to break down and call a farrier. Mackenzie
grilled him on the phone…asked him all sorts of technical
questions about balance and angles and heel length. Poor guy.
It must be tough to work for someone who probably knows
more than you do. But Mackenzie had noticed that some of the
shoes had gotten loose. We agreed that we would have the
new guy just pull the shoes off and trim them all up. It had

been easier for her to keep front shoes on all of her horses. But we wanted to see how this farrier did before we had him do any shoeing.

Lester pulled into the driveway in his shoeing rig. It was a three-quarter ton pickup with a trailer towed behind. His skinny wife got out and helped him set up all his tools. It looked like a hardware store on wheels. He even had his own power source. And he had a drill press, several grinders, a propane forge, and a huge anvil that slid out from under the truck like a submarine that had been launched from a secret cave. I wondered how much all that equipment had cost. And I marveled that this young couple could have afforded it all. Mackenzie talked shop with him from a distance. But he had evidently been born without a personality. So had his wife. That must have been what drew them together. She held each horse while her husband worked. Mackenzie and I tried to make small talk. It was as impossible as stirring concrete…concrete that has already set.

Talking shop proved even more difficult for Mackenzie. The guy could not even remember where he'd gone to horseshoeing school. He would have been better off to just admit that he had not gone to school. Mackenzie told me later that many horseshoers learn the trade by apprenticing with a relative. There's no shame in that. But his credibility had been greatly diminished by an obvious lie. Plus, he treated the horses like they were inanimate objects. And he trimmed them all the same. After he left, Mackenzie felt a few hooves. We decided not to ask him back.

My objection to the man was that he littered the barn isle with nails. The bent little nails that he'd pulled or allowed to fall from the discarded old shoes. Sloppy. Especially since my Mackenzie had always been so tidy when she'd done the same work. Exacting standards. So we decided to interview potential candidates for future use.

The first guy reeked of machismo. Scout tried to kick him when he yanked his foot up off the ground to look at it. When the horse kicked, the guy yelled at the horse and called him a 'Puke.' I thought Mackenzie was going to come unglued.

161

Having been in the corporate world, I wasn't familiar with that term. But I knew it wasn't a favorable one.

"Who the hell do you think you are.... manhandling my horse!" Mackenzie fumed. "Get off my property before I call the Sheriff." She shoved him towards his truck. "You're the 'puke' here.... that horse has never kicked at anyone...but I have." I laughed under my breath. And I hoped I wouldn't have to break up a fight.

The guy was cussing and calling us names as he drove down the driveway spinning the tires on his monster Chevy truck. Really professional. We fired him. Mackenzie explained that people in the horse world use the term 'puke' to describe an obnoxious or worthless horse. Scout was far from fitting that description. I hated it when people blamed their ineptness on a horse. He was too rough with the horse and we were glad Scout had offered to kick. Too bad he'd missed.

This other guy came highly recommended by the vet. He was supposed to be a specialist of some kind and that was the name that Clayton gave out any time someone called his office looking for a farrier. When Mackenzie asked about his 'specialty' he didn't seem to know what she was talking about...had only worked on one horse with that ailment. The vet was only recommending him because he was part of the good ole boy network. Mackenzie was all too familiar with that mentality. When you are a male horseshoer you seldom have to prove yourself. As a woman in a man's world, professionals assume that you must not know very much. When Mackenzie had first started shoeing horses, Clayton had assumed that she didn't own a forge. How could a woman know how to use one of those contraptions? Just because Mackenzie does not have every tool known to man people had assumed she had nothing. Including the knowledge to shoe horses with foot problems. Plus her rig never was a tool shop on wheels. A truck, an anvil, and her hand tools were all she had needed. She had a forge at home that was gathering dust right along with all the rest of her shoeing paraphernalia.

We finally settled on the best of the worst. But we wouldn't need to call him for at least two months. Now that all of our horses were barefoot, we would need a farrier less often. That seemed like a good thing since the choices were limited here. Mackenzie seemed frustrated by it all. When Becca heard that someone had called Scout a 'puke' she was livid. Called the guy up right away and attempted to set him straight. He hung up on her. Some people see no need to learn anything in life. For us, we were learning that there are all sorts of adjustments in life and all sorts of horse people out there. And we missed Mackenzie's role as our farrier. Her new role as their equine massage therapist would come soon enough. And she was practicing her technique on us all. Willing subjects.

TWENTY-SIX: Wedding Bells

The day had finally arrived! The sun rose strong on our wedding day. April fifteenth. While other people were scrambling to get their income tax returns completed and filed, Mackenzie and I were preparing to get married. Too bad that the great state of Georgia does not see fit to recognize same-sex marriages. Maybe that day will come. But for Mackenzie and me, as well as all of our friends and family who had assembled, this was the real deal. This was my second trip down the isle...real or unsanctioned. It was Mackenzie's first. For everyone here, except the minister who was officiating, this was our first gay wedding ceremony.

Both of our mothers were noticeably nervous. I haven't checked, but I doubt that any book of etiquette has a chapter on the proper rules of decorum for a same-sex wedding. And it showed on the faces of some who were present. That tentative and uncomfortable smile shows an uncertainty about all this letting-your-hair-down-in-public lesbianism. But it was evident to all present that Mackenzie and I loved each other very much. Everybody also knew that we belonged together. This ceremony was only an outward declaration of what everyone knew to be true...including the two of us.

I didn't think I would be nervous this time. For my first wedding I had been so nervous that applying makeup had been a problem. This time I wore none. But when I was combing Mackenzie's silken black hair, I noticed that my hand was trembling.

"Nervous, my dear?" She both noticed my trembling and asked about it calmly.

"Yeah," I admitted. "And I didn't think I would be this time." I observed out loud.

"Getting cold feet?" Mackenzie asked.

"Not a chance." I replied with both words and a long slow kiss that reinforced my feelings about marrying her. "How 'bout you?" I asked. I only had a fleeting worry even though Mackenzie had long ago spelled out her fear of marriage.

"No Sandy." She said with a certain smile. "You're the woman of my dreams, and I want nothing more than to be your wife this day." She punctuated her declaration with a kiss as I had done. There is nothing that compares to the way a woman kisses you when she loves you with all her being. I had been kissed by a man in a similar situation. This was entirely different. Closer. She pulled me near. As we breathed in unison, I knew without a doubt that this marriage was right. "I just wish I could see my beautiful bride." As she spoke a tear slipped from her eye.

"Hey…no crying today…and no regrets." I admonished as I swept the tear from her face with a handkerchief. "You should see how good you look, too." I added. We wore similar custom-tailored pants suits. Mine was black and hers was white. Both had long suit coats that fit well. Mackenzie looked like a model with her jet-black hair and blue eyes emerging from the crisp white material. Her pale blue shirt was exactly the color of her eyes. And it was unbuttoned a little too far. I could hardly stand it. Our blue shirts and black dress shoes were the only things exactly the same. We each had on a hand-made blue garter that the other would remove later and throw to the crowd. And we each had a bouquet of tulips, daffodils, and ivy that we would toss those aspiring to marry. We were not men and we were neither dressing like men for this occasion nor acting like men. But neither of us wanted to wear a dress. Pants were a compromise.

"I have never been more certain of anything in my life." I told Mackenzie as I penned the narcissus and ivy boutonniere on her lapel. She looked stunning. This time alone we were sharing before our wedding ceremony was priceless. Only during sex had I ever felt this close to her. But I had not expected to be this nervous. My hands still shook.

"That's how I feel, too." Mackenzie said, "But there's something I want you to know before we go out there."

"I knew it…you're really a man!" I joked.

"Now you know better than that." She smiled seductively. Then her brows furrowed. She took both my hands in hers and spoke. "I want you to know that I'm doing this because I'm in love with you...not because I'm blind and in need of somebody to look after me."

"I know that, Honey." I said. "You proved that point a long time ago."

"I just want you to be sure of it." Mackenzie said with the most sincerity I had ever seen on her face. "I wanted to marry you the instant our lips touched for the first time. I wanted that moment to last forever. I wanted this day..." She finished.

It was a good thing that neither of us was wearing makeup because tears streamed down both of our faces as she spoke. Remembering our first kiss was so tender and touching. We felt the same way. We had reunited soul mates and planned to seal it with a ceremony of marriage. Memories of falling in love are so important to any marriage. Ours will sustain us in the coming years together.

A soft knock on the door interrupted us. "You ladies about ready in there?" Becca's voice was friendly, as usual.

"Come in." We spoke in unison.

"Wow, look at you two...what a handsome couple!" She declared as she caught sight of us. Becca had always acted so natural about our relationship. She'd even fought for it. Most people who are against same-sex unions are threatened by their own sexuality, I think. This woman was sure of herself...and of us. It was refreshing.

"You look pretty smart yourself." I said to Becca. She had on a pale blue linen suit. Even though she was blind, Mackenzie had been involved in coordinating the color schemes and the flower choices. It had all come together so well. I wished she could see all that for herself.

"It's show time." Becca said.

"We're ready...except for this." I replied as I handed Becca my boutonniere. She pinned it in place on my lapel. After a final hair and zipper check, we were ready to emerge. Becca led Mackenzie to the front near the minister and I found my spot at the corner of the house. We had rented a wooden archway and a green carpet split the rows of folding chairs that held our guests. The minister was a woman from a church in Atlanta. Not many churches sanction same-sex unions. Reverend Morris was a woman who was about my mother's age. She smiled broadly when Mackenzie was brought to a stop. So did Pam, a friend of Mackenzie's from horseshoeing school. Pam elbowed Mackenzie and whispered something to her that made my bride laugh. Pam's husband in the audience laughed, as well...he must have heard. We had made it clear to all concerned that we were both brides. There was no husband in this ceremony. Some lesbians try to mimic traditional roles and wear tuxedos and act manly. While that is okay for them, we wanted something less forced. We just wanted to be together and to have a ceremony to proclaim that.

My mother was sitting on the front row on the left. She had expressed long ago that she was not at all pleased about the 'situation', as she called my relationship with Mackenzie. But she'd agreed to attend. Beverly Coleman was poised on the other side of the isle at front in her seat of honor. Becca stood up front with us...as did Tim. I'd never seen him dressed up. He was beaming with pride. Barb, my friend since high school was up front waiting for my arrival, as well. The music alerted everyone that I was coming down the isle. Butterflies swarmed in my stomach. But the sight of Mackenzie gave me focus. As I stopped, Reverend Morris began to speak.

"Dear friends and loved ones: We are gathered here today to witness the union of these two women we all love. Mackenzie Coleman and Sandra Greene are here today to pledge their love for each other in marriage. Love is precious in the sight of our Lord. All love. Though this love is not understood or sanctioned by all, it is considered holy by our church....and by our God, the source of all love." As she spoke she looked both at the two of us and occasionally at the audience. "At this time Sandy and Mackenzie would like to read some quotations that refer to this love they feel for each other." I had chosen a Shakespearian sonnet, and cleared my throat to begin reading.

"When, in disgrace with Fortune and men's eyes,

I all alone beweep my outcast state,

And trouble deaf heaven with my bootless cries,

And look upon myself and curse my fate,

Wishing me like to one more rich in hope,

Featured like him, like him with friends possessed,

Desiring this man's art, and that man's scope,

With what I most enjoy contented least;

Yet in these thoughts myself almost despising,

Haply, I think on thee, and then my state,

Like to the lark at break of day arising

From sullen earth, sings hymns at heaven's gate;

For thy sweet love rememb'red such wealth brings,

That then I scorn to change my state with kings."

I added to the words of the Bard. "This is how I feel for you, Mackenzie. Your love makes me feel wealthy. And your presence in my life makes my spirit take flight. I wouldn't change places with anyone right now…especially on this day that marks the official union of our lives. This is a day I have dreamed about all my life. You are the love of my life and I thank you for choosing to love me. Thank you for agreeing to be my wife."

As I spoke I could trace tears glistening their way down Mackenzie's face. She pulled a linen handkerchief from her pocket and dabbed them away with a smile. After I finished, the minister asked Mackenzie if she had anything to share. She began quoting from memory the words from a Wynonna song,

"Love that's worth fighting for

That's what this is

And how, how could I want more

Than the warmth of your kiss...

Let the mountains rise, I will climb them all.

In Another Life

When my body's weak, I will not fall.

Baby come what may, I will find a way to get through

There's nothing I won't do

To be loved by you.

Should every star in the sky go out

Just keep your faith alive

We were meant to be, this is destiny

It cannot be denied."

Then Mackenzie found my face with both of her hands. She spoke to me as if we were all alone. "I love you, Sandy." By now there wasn't a dry eye in the crowd. Even big ole Tim was teary-eyed. Only people who feel love can be moved to tears by witnessing this sort of ceremony. "When I met you, I began to see something as clear as the darkness that surrounds me now. I saw a remarkable strong intelligent woman. And I saw myself longing to be near you as often as I could. I saw my heart tumble uncontrollably towards you. I saw you look at me like my grandmamma looked at my granddaddy." With those words, she choked. She steadied her jaw and continued, "And I felt myself looking back. I have fallen in love with you, Sandy. I want to share life with you…all the life we have before us. I pledge to love you in every way until death parts us. Thank you for loving me…and for agreeing to be my wife…on this glorious day!" As she finished her smile was so strong that it looked as if it might cause her face to break off just under her ears.

"Let us now proceed with the scripture readings and the vows." The minister spoke with conviction. "I will first paraphrase and then read from the book of Ruth in the Old Testament. In the days in which there was no king in Israel, the judges ruled. There lived then a woman named Naomi, whose husband and two sons died, probably as the result of a famine. After their deaths, Naomi urged her two daughters-in-law to return to their homes and seek out new husbands. One did so. But Ruth hung onto Naomi and said, 'Entreat me not to leave thee, or to return

169

from following after thee: for whither thou goest, I will go; and where thou lodgest, I will lodge: thy people will be my people, and thy God, my God: Where thou diest, will I die, and there will I be buried: the Lord do so to me, and more also, if aut but death part thee and me.' As you can see, some relationships are meant to be permanent. Sandra and Mackenzie have come together to proclaim that their union is to be a permanent one. Let us now witness the exchange of vows. Do you have rings?" She asked.

"We do." Mackenzie and I spoke in unison as we fumbled for the rings. Becca had them both tucked away in separate pockets.

"Good. Please face each other as you pledge your love," The minister instructed as she spoke. I had heard this ceremony many times, but it meant so much more now that I felt the presence of Mackenzie's affection. I'd even been a bride before. It felt nothing like this.

"Sandra, do you take Mackenzie to be your wife…to have and to hold, for richer for poorer, for better for worse, in sickness and in health, to face all of life's joys and sorrows giving yourself only unto her until death do you part?" Asked the minister.

"I do." I answered with firmness and a smile.

"Mackenzie, do you take Sandra to be your wife…to have and to hold, for richer for poorer, for better for worse, in sickness and in health, to face all of life's joys and sorrows giving yourself only unto her until death do you part?" She repeated.

"I do." Mackenzie said, as she stood up taller.

"Then will both of you place the ring on the left hand of your wife and repeat after me…with this ring, I thee wed." She spoke and we repeated her words. "Accept and wear it as a reminder of our marriage to you and to the world." As we spoke the words I was so proud. And amazed that such a remarkable woman had fallen in love with me. Married me! After we repeated the vows, the minister gave us permission, "You may seal your vows with a kiss."

With that, Mackenzie took my face in her hands and kissed me long and steadily and convincingly. Everybody laughed and cried at the same time.

"Let us now celebrate this union!" The minister stretched out her arms to us all as she spoke. Everyone clapped. If my heart had gotten any fuller it might have burst right out of my chest.

As we stood facing each other kissing and wiping away tears of joy, the photographer snapped a picture. I silently wished it could frame up all that love for all the world to see. I knew I would always be able to recall anew the knot of happy emotions that had woven itself into my chest. Hopefully Mackenzie felt this good. From the look on her face I knew she did. We toasted each other and greeted our guests. Everyone was feeling festive. Even our mothers danced to the songs and seemed sincerely happy for us.

Rice pelted us both in the faces as we ducked into the car to head for the airport. From the air I described the sunset to Mackenzie. Jekyll Island was awash in orange. As our plane touched down, I longed to be alone with my bride. The festivities had been fun, but I needed her. We needed this. In the morning, we could have coffee in bed and walk on the beach. Tonight I had other things in mind.

This was our honeymoon. And we had reserved the Honeymoon Suite. Strange looks from the desk clerk.

"You guess we're the first lesbians to have this suite?" I asked Mackenzie.

"I hope so." She said as she slammed the door. "Take off your clothes, woman."

"Awfully demanding, aren't you?" I said pretending to pout.

"No…I'm begging." She said as she pulled me close and helped me out of my clothes. "I wanna taste you…" She whispered with a groan in my ear.

"I've wanted this all day." I admitted as her sleek pants crumpled on the floor. She kicked off the shoes while I unbuttoned her shirt and kissed her back. I bit now and then.

At last we were both naked and standing…holding each other close.

"Point me to the bed, please." She requested.

I obliged and she pulled me down on top of her just like I had done that first time. Candles and champagne and flowers were all there in that hotel suite as requested. We never lit the candles. And we didn't pour the champagne until much later.

The only time I'd ever been this sexually excited was the day I had invited her to come over to my house early in the morning. This time there was neither awkwardness nor hesitation. It was all familiar. It was perfect. And it was all night. We barely slept. When we did it was sweet.

The rest of our honeymoon was relaxing. We went for long walks hand in hand on the moonlit beach. We had breakfast in bed. Collecting shells or napping under the umbrella…we were always touching each other. We enjoyed this luxury although it felt weird to be away from all our animals. Becca and Tim were looking after the Plan B. And Doc Thompson knew we were away on our honeymoon. My dates with him seemed like a lifetime ago. He had come to the wedding. Spending all that time with Mackenzie made me even more certain that our marriage was right. And seeing my ring on her finger made me proud.

I watched the sun sink into the ocean in a pastel blur on our last night at the beach. Mid-morning the next day, we boarded our plane for the trip home. Our life together was comfortable. Our daily routines would continue. We took a taxi home from the airport, and Mitch greeted us on the trip down the driveway. He was a great dog. It seemed like he'd always been mine. So did Mackenzie. It was good to be back home.

It was good to be married. When I returned home from my first marriage I'd been certain I had made an egregious error. This time I was sure I had begun the best chapter of my life thus far.

TWENTY-SEVEN: Returning Favors

The phone awakened us both. It was early morning but still dark. Becca's voice on the other end of the phone sounded tense and afraid. "Sandy…can y'all come over and help me…the baby is down and it's a bad colic." She was unsuccessfully fighting back tears.

"Of course." I assured her. "We'll be right there." Mackenzie heard my side of the conversation and had already gotten up and begun dressing. I threw on my clothes and retrieved her cane.

"Let me hold you on the way over." Mackenzie requested. "It'll be faster that way."

Becca's Appaloosa mare had foaled about a month and a half after my arrival from the city. She was now almost two years old. Becca had handled her since the minute she hit the ground, so she was tame as a puppy. Her coat was white with small black spots, which is known as a leopard Appaloosa. Very beautiful. But now she was a very sick filly. Becca needed our help because Tim was still at work. Horses seem to want to roll on the ground when they have a stomachache. That can cause their gut to twist, and they die easily that way. We would have to keep the filly on her feet. Or at least prevent her from rolling violently on the ground. When they are in a great deal of pain, that can be an almost impossible task.

When we arrived, Becca was pulling with all her might on the lead line. The filly wasn't budging. Her ears pointed straight out to the side and she was covered with sweat and dirt. She'd been rolling. This didn't look good, at all.

Mackenzie had trouble getting her bearings, but she insisted on helping. "Let's get her up and out of this paddock…so the mare won't be in our way." Her idea was a good one.

"Sorry to get you two up so early." Becca said apologetically.

"No problem." I replied.

"Part of being friends." Mackenzie added.

Once we were able to get her up onto her wobbly legs
and out of the paddock, we began walking her in a big circle.
However, she could only take a few steps before her legs
seemed to turn into lead underneath her slim body. Legs
buckled and down she went with a thud! Mackenzie helped us
whoop, holler, and slap until we could convince her to stand
again. Waiting for the vet seemed interminable. Becca had
told us that Clayton was already treating another colic and
would be here as soon as possible. The sun was trying to come
up by now and dew had settled on us all. The filly was
shivering.

Becca had given her a shot of Banamine to settle her stomach,
but nothing seemed to help…not even the constant walking.
Mackenzie periodically listened for gut sounds on both sides of
the horse. She heard nothing except labored breathing. Horses
are always supposed to have gurgling noises inside. The filly's
little nostrils flared as she breathed hard and blinked the blinks
that show pain. Becca let her stop to rest now and then and
talked softly to her. I had never seen it done before, but I'd
read about how the vet can pump mineral oil into a tube that
runs in the horse's nose and to the stomach. That helps get
them unclogged. We prayed for his arrival.

Just as Doc Thompson's truck turned into the driveway, the
filly went down hard. This time was different. It was all at
once. Her legs gave way and she fell onto her side. She
breathed hard and groaned. Then her eyes locked in place.

"NO!" Becca screamed. However, with all her years as a nurse
she knew the finality of that stare. Clayton knew too. As soon
as his truck stopped and he stepped into the spotlight the
headlights had created, he knew. His stethoscope confirmed it.
The horse was dead.

Becca buried her face in the little horse's silky white mane and
cried. We all did too. Even the vet cried. He'd lost the other
horse earlier, too. It all seemed too much to bear. Especially
losing a baby. The mare now knew it, as well. She stopped
grazing and screamed a command of sorts to her lifeless
offspring. That made it worse. Clayton apologized for not
being able to get there sooner. Becca understood.

"When will Tim be home?" I asked.

"Around 7:30 unless he has to work over." Becca sputtered. She'd always been there for us. During the hours and days right after Mackenzie's accident, she had been my fortress. Now, as I stood there trying to console her somehow, I had to draw on a reserve of strength from somewhere deep inside myself. This was awful.

Clayton tried to reassure Becca. The filly had probably been sick and rolling all throughout the night. She wouldn't have made it anyway, even if he'd been able to get there right away. Even surgery might not have helped since the gases that build up inside a horse had already done their damage.

"There's a tarp over there." Becca cried uncontrollably now. "I hate seeing her this way." As we were stretching the tarp out over the horse, Tim pulled into the driveway. The sun was up now, and the look that overtook his face as he became aware of what was happening was horrible to see. His eyes darted frantically from horse to horse before he realized that it was the baby there underneath the tarp we were spreading. Before his big feet hit the Georgia clay, he was bawling like a baby.

"What happened?" He managed to ask the question through all the tears.

"Colic." That was all Becca was able to say before his arms enveloped her. We all stood there and cried. Then Tim resolutely walked towards the tractor. He was going to dig the hole. Becca stood there crying as she pointed to the proper spot. He nodded and began to dig. All we could do was to hold each other and cry along with our friend. There is nothing you can say to someone at a time like that. But this was our turn to help Becca. Now as we stood there in the dawn, while her husband buried her baby horse, we only wished that the outcome had been different for her. We wished there was some way to comfort her in this loss. We did our best.

The entire incident was gut wrenching. We could hardly even speak about it for days. Constant contact with Becca helped her as much as anything could. Death is such a final thing.

But Becca planned to breed the mare again. We all
knew that even another similar baby couldn't replace the one
she had lost. Lacy was a unique girl and we could sense the
depth of Becca's grief. Losing a horse is a horrible
thing…even when they are old. This had blindsided us all.

We invited Becca and Tim over for dinner in an extra effort to
take their minds off the loss. Our conversation led to horses
and breeding. Becca was glad we had babies on the way. New
life makes grief less pronounced, and even though they were
our horses, Becca felt like she was family. She was…they both
were. These people had become so dear to me. My life had
taken such a turn since I had moved back to Georgia. My path
had been like the one that Robert Frost writes about in a poem,
"Two paths diverged in the woods, and I took the one less
traveled by…and that has made all the difference." I could no
longer picture myself as a city dweller. Nor could I picture
myself with anyone except Mackenzie. I was no longer the
same woman. It saddened me to know that many people never
realize their dreams as I had. They never have the courage to
act. And they certainly didn't have the openness to find love in
an unexpected person. I had it all and I vowed not to take any
of it for granted.

Each day when I awoke with Mackenzie, I thanked her for
being in my life. And I tried not to take even the smallest
things for granted. I had my home, my animals, my wife, my
crops, and my horse farm. Plan B was going according to plan.
The summer that followed seemed even better than the
previous one since Mackenzie and I now lived in the same
house. Her accident had served to weld us together. Through
fire. Now it was hard to imagine that she'd ever lived
anywhere else.

Princess Jazmine was the herald. She waited each morning to
see movement in the cabin. She whinnied early one morning
and I decided we should ride. The weather was perfect. We
shared our coffee on the porch. That had become one of our
intimate morning rituals. Mackenzie had also learned to do a
respectable job of saddling her horse even though she couldn't
see. Scout seemed to stand better for her as time went by. The

sun was warming things up. All the smells of coffee, earth, and horses. Our lovemaking earlier. We were basking in it all as we rode and I thought that this was a perfect way for a day to unfold.

"Hey, this is where we went that time…" I reflected as my horse stepped in the river.

"That time you gawked at my breast." Mackenzie laughed as she spoke.

"Yeah, and drooled would be a better choice of words." I agreed.

We had taken that path long ago and both of our horses were now in the river. The horses splashed water on us both with their legs. Spring rains had been frequent and the river was full. It looked inviting.

"Hold on." I said. I jumped off Princess Jazmine and the water came up to my waist. And I had an idea. I let my horse go and reached for Scout.

"Wanna play in the water?" I said as I put my arm around Mackenzie's waist. "Like we did that one day?" She agreed, so I unclipped the reins from both of our horses. They were not going anywhere and neither were we. I kissed her and she knew just what I wanted. Right there in the river we opened our clothes and our hearts to each other. The horses afforded us our privacy. Fortunately, they didn't run away. It would have been a long walk home. The water felt almost cold. Just as it had been that first time long ago when I watched it trickle its way down Mackenzie's pretty face. I could no longer imagine my life without her. As I kissed her, I felt so full and I tried to convey gratitude in my kiss. She seemed to sense the emotions that spilled out of me like the overflowing river we were sitting in.

Mackenzie relaxed in my arms and sighed. She looked up at me and said, "That green shirt goes well with your hair." But I saw a tear. About the time I wondered why she was crying and how she knew that the shirt I was putting back on was green, she screamed, "I CAN SEE!" Standing there dripping wet in

the river she was looking directly into my eyes with
that long lost recognition I had missed. No longer did she have
that glazed stare of the blind. She was back.

"What do you mean, you can see?" I shouted too!

"I mean I can see. I can see everything!" She was crying,
shouting, and laughing all at the same time. "I can see your
pretty eyes, and your green shirt, and the blue sky, and
everything. I can see it all and it all looks so bright." As she
spoke, she squinted. I had held out hope for this moment. The
doctors said this might happen. It felt like a really vivid dream.
It wasn't. Mackenzie had regained her sight. I grabbed her up
and held her close and we cried tears of joy together right there
in the river where it all began. Our lovemaking had been so
intense. This put us way over the top. We sat down on the
bank in the wet sand and just held each other while she looked
around.

"I missed this." She said as she took in the sights. "And I
hope it doesn't go away again." She added.

"The doctors said this might happen…remember?" I reminded
her of what all the doctors had said.

"I know…but I had given up hope." She admitted.

"Just goes to show you, you never know what the future
holds." I philosophized. "I never knew I would be lucky
enough to meet you and fall in love with you…and have you
love me, too."

"I'll never take any of this for granted." She said as she pulled
me close. We hugged and kissed. She stared into my eyes
with that look that only she had for me. And I looked back
with mine. Even though I was sure of her love for me, it felt
good to once again see it at home in her eyes.

We finished dressing and gathered in our horses. They seemed
to feel our exuberance. We swung back onto our horses. The
rope for ponying her wasn't needed anymore and hung limply
around Scout's neck. I clipped it to my saddle. Mackenzie led
and we proceeded at a leisurely walk. Then she stopped her
horse, turned around, and winked. "Race you home!" She

shouted. The mischievous grin on her face explained it all. However, we both knew that my horse was faster than Scout was. After about two hundred yards, we passed her. As we did so, I slowed my horse and smiled. I held out my hand to her in knightly fashion. And m'lady took my hand and held it tightly as we rode the rest of the way home. I wished I could hold onto her forever that way. I wished that moment and or at least that feeling could last forever. It felt like it just might.

I knew we would face adversity in the days that lay ahead. This high we felt right now would wane. But we both knew we would face all of the bends in life's road together. It had all come into focus. Plan C.

THE END

ABOUT THE AUTHOR

Meg Oliver is a Vidalia, Georgia native. She lives and writes in Cheyenne, Wyoming. She is a graduate of the University of Florida, Kentucky Horseshoeing School, and The Institute of Business and Medical Careers. She is a retired Farrier of fifteen years and a practicing Massage Therapist. She is currently horseless, but she shares her home with her family, which includes many dogs and cats. If you have questions or comments about the book or books-in-progress, you may write Meg at OliverOptions@yahoo.com or visit the book's website at http://stores.lulu.com/oliveroptions

Every report card Meg ever received said, "talks too much." That was a talent yet to be discovered! Thanks for reading.

In Another Life